THE DARK SIDE OF PHILANTHROPY

HOW CHARITABLE FOUNDATIONS ENABLE POWER CONSOLIDATION

Dr. Karthik Karunakaran, Ph.D.

Copyright © 2024 by Karthik Karunakaran.

All rights reserved. No part of this book may be used or reproduced in any form whatsoever without written permission except in the case of brief quotations in critical articles or reviews.

Printed in the United States of America.

For more information, or to book an event, contact :
karthikk@alumni.iitm.ac.in

CONTENTS

1. THE DARK SIDE OF PHILANTHROPY: HOW CHARITABLE FOUNDATIONS BECOME TOOLS FOR POWER CONSOLIDATION

2. THE HISTORICAL ROOTS OF ELITE PHILANTHROPY: FROM THE GILDED AGE TO MODERN POWER CONSOLIDATION

3. THE CHARITABLE PARADOX: HOW FOUNDATIONS SHELTER WEALTH WHILE PRESERVING POWER

4. THE MEDIA'S PHILANTHROPIC LENS: SHAPING PUBLIC PERCEPTION TO FAVOR THE ELITE

5. STRATEGIC PHILANTHROPY: THE HIDDEN INFLUENCE OF WEALTH ON SOCIETY'S PRIORITIES

6. CORPORATE PHILANTHROPY: THE HIDDEN AGENDA BEHIND BRAND GOODWILL

7. PHILANTHROPIC POWER: HOW CHARITABLE FOUNDATIONS SHAPE POLICY FOR PRIVATE GAIN

8. THE PRICE OF KNOWLEDGE: HOW PHILANTHROPIC DONATIONS SHAPE EDUCATION, MARGINALISE THE UNDERSERVED, AND PRIORITISE THE ELITE

9. THE POLITICS OF AID: HOW LARGE FOUNDATIONS SHAPE DEVELOPMENT IN THE GLOBAL SOUTH

10. THE CHARITABLE ILLUSION: HOW DONATIONS MASK THE HARMFUL PRACTICES OF THE HEALTHCARE INDUSTRY

11. THE GREEN MIRAGE: HOW ENVIRONMENTAL PHILANTHROPIES SHIELD POLLUTERS AND STUNT REAL CLIMATE ACTION

12. THE PARADOX OF POWER: HOW LARGE NONPROFITS BECOME TOOLS FOR THE ELITES THEY WERE MEANT TO CHALLENGE

13. THE PROFIT MOTIVE IN SCIENCE: HOW CHARITABLE FOUNDATIONS SHAPE RESEARCH AND INNOVATION

14. DYNASTIES OF GENEROSITY: HOW ELITE FAMILIES PRESERVE

POWER THROUGH CHARITABLE GIVING

15. THE ILLUSION OF BENEVOLENCE: HOW SMALL CHARITABLE GESTURES DISTRACT FROM HARMFUL PRACTICES

16. CHALLENGING THE MONOPOLY OF ELITE PHILANTHROPY: THE RISE OF GRASSROOTS MOVEMENTS AND ALTERNATIVE MODELS

17. PHILANTHROPY AT A CROSSROADS: REFORMING CHARITY TO SERVE THE PUBLIC GOOD

ABOUT THE AUTHOR

CHAPTER 1

THE DARK SIDE OF PHILANTHROPY: HOW CHARITABLE FOUNDATIONS BECOME TOOLS FOR POWER CONSOLIDATION

Philanthropy is often seen as the purest form of altruism—a giving hand extended to uplift the downtrodden, heal the sick, and enrich the lives of those less fortunate. At its best, it can do all these things. But philanthropy harbours a more complex and often insidious reality behind the veneer of benevolence. Wealthy individuals and corporations, through charitable foundations, can shape public perception of their "goodwill" and strategically consolidate power, influence policies, and safeguard their interests.

The Illusion of Altruism

In today's world, charity has become synonymous with progress. Foundations like the Bill and Melinda Gates Foundation or the Chan Zuckerberg Initiative embody a moral commitment to global betterment. They fight pandemics, improve educational outcomes, and work to eliminate poverty. These efforts are unquestionably admirable from a distance, but when examined closely, cracks in this utopian narrative begin to appear.

At the heart of the issue lies the structure of charitable foundations themselves. They provide a way for the ultra-wealthy to shield vast sums of money from taxation while expanding their influence. The world's billionaires can set up foundations, donate to them, and receive enormous tax deductions. The foundations then distribute a portion of the wealth toward causes the benefactors deem worthy—often reinforcing their ideological, economic, or political interests.

This is the first layer of control: dictating the terms of charity. The public believes that the wealthy are giving back, but in reality, these individuals are deciding which issues are essential, which policies to fund, and which narratives to promote. It's an invisible steering mechanism where power flows outward, disguised as goodwill.

Philanthropy as a Mechanism for Policy Influence

Philanthropy has also become a powerful vehicle for influencing public policy. Consider how large foundations affect global health. The Gates Foundation, for example, has poured billions into fighting diseases such as malaria and HIV/AIDS. While these efforts have made a difference, they also highlight a troubling trend. With their vast resources, these foundations have an outsized influence on health priorities worldwide, often in ways that align with corporate interests.

The agenda-setting power of these foundations means that public health priorities can be swayed to favour certain pharmaceutical companies, reinforce intellectual property rights that prevent affordable medicine access, or prioritise diseases that primarily affect markets valuable to wealthy nations. This influence creates a conflict: whose interests are being served when policies are written to accommodate donors' priorities?

Even in areas like education, charitable contributions come with invisible strings. When wealthy benefactors funnel money into school systems or university research programs, they often subtly shape curricula, research agendas, or hiring practices to benefit their own businesses or ideologies. Educational funding has transformed from a public good into a privatised tool of influence.

The Politics of Philanthropy

If we look deeper, it becomes clear that philanthropy is not only an instrument of policy manipulation but also a mechanism for reinforcing and expanding power through political influence. Wealthy donors frequently use foundations to bankroll political campaigns or influence elections, often bypassing campaign finance restrictions. By supporting think tanks, media outlets, and lobbying groups, these foundations create and amplify political narratives that protect their interests, be it lower corporate taxes, deregulation, or global trade policies favourable to multinational corporations.

An often-cited example is the Koch brothers' extensive network of philanthropic giving, which has significantly shaped American political discourse. Through their donations, they have nurtured a sprawling network of organisations promoting free-market ideologies and anti-regulation policies. While these contributions are cloaked in the language of "defending individual liberties" or "fostering economic growth," they serve a singular purpose: to ensure that the interests of the wealthy are preserved at the expense of the broader public.

This is not to suggest that all philanthropic giving is rooted in nefarious intent but rather to illuminate the undeniable fact that the wealthy—through their foundations—exert influence on political landscapes in ways that the average citizen cannot.

Safeguarding Power and Image

There is another side to this story: reputation. In the age of social media, public perception is everything. Corporations and individuals alike use philanthropy to whitewash their public image. After all, how can you criticise a corporation when its name is plastered across children's hospitals or a billionaire whose foundation has provided clean water to impoverished nations?

Corporate social responsibility programs and philanthropic donations are buffers against public criticism and scandals. Environmental disasters caused by corporations, exploitative labour practices, or unethical business dealings are quickly swept under the rug when paired with apparent charitable efforts. Companies present themselves as socially responsible actors, and individuals with questionable business practices suddenly transform into altruistic figures.

The Power Imbalance in Global Development

Finally, philanthropy in the developing world highlights the stark power imbalance perpetuated by wealthy foundations. When these foundations donate to countries in Africa, Latin America, or Asia, they often create a paternalistic dynamic in which local governments and communities are accountable to the will of their benefactors. It is not uncommon for these foundations to undermine local governance by insisting on implementing specific programs or reforms that align with their vision, regardless of the unique needs or desires of the communities they claim to help.

In doing so, philanthropy strips these regions of agency, turning them into laboratories for the wealthy to experiment with ideas, policies, or technologies that often perpetuate dependence rather than foster actual, sustainable development. Wealthy donors take on the role of decision-makers, overshadowing the voices of those they are supposedly serving.

CHAPTER 2

THE HISTORICAL ROOTS OF ELITE PHILANTHROPY: FROM THE GILDED AGE TO MODERN POWER CONSOLIDATION

In the late 19th century, America was swept into unprecedented wealth and transformation. The Industrial Revolution had given rise to titans of industry—men whose names, like Rockefeller, Carnegie, and Vanderbilt, would become synonymous with capitalism and affluence. This period, known as the Gilded Age, was marked by staggering economic growth and rampant inequality, corruption, and exploitation. Amid the vast fortunes accumulated by these industrialists, another story began to unfold—one of strategic philanthropy.

The roots of elite philanthropy, as we understand it today, can be traced to this era, when industrial magnates began to use charitable giving not only to burnish their public image but also to secure influence and manage public perception. By presenting themselves as benevolent figures, these elites sought to mitigate the social unrest their business practices often incited, creating a legacy that would endure far beyond their lifetimes.

The Birth of the Industrial Titans

The Gilded Age industrialists—Andrew Carnegie, John D. Rockefeller, Cornelius Vanderbilt, and others—built America's new economic order. They controlled vast swaths of the economy, from oil and steel to railroads and finance. Their fortunes were built on monopolistic practices, labour exploitation, and aggressive business tactics that crushed competition and often harmed workers.

Yet, as their wealth grew, so did public resentment. By the late 19th century, inequality had reached staggering levels, with a small elite controlling much of the nation's wealth while the working class toiled in dangerous conditions for paltry wages. Labour strikes, protests, and calls for reform were becoming increasingly common, threatening the stability of the industrialists' empires. These captains of industry recognised the need to address their public image and stave off the growing societal unrest. Enter philanthropy.

Andrew Carnegie: The Gospel of Wealth

One of the most prominent figures in the history of elite philanthropy was Andrew Carnegie, a Scottish-born steel magnate whose rise to wealth epitomised the American Dream. Carnegie's wealth was staggering; at his peak, he was one of the wealthiest men in the world. However, his legacy was not merely built on his fortune but also on his philosophy of giving.

In 1889, Carnegie published his famous essay, The Gospel of Wealth, which outlined his belief that the wealthy had a moral obligation to give back to society. Carnegie argued that those who accumulated great wealth were merely stewards of that wealth, and it was their duty to use it for the greater good. However, he also made clear that philanthropy should be deployed strategically. Rather than simply giving money to people experiencing poverty, Carnegie believed that wealth should be used to create opportunities for self-improvement—through libraries, universities, and cultural institutions.

This was a radical shift from the more traditional forms of charity, which often focused on direct aid to people experiencing poverty. Carnegie's approach emphasised the empowerment of individuals through education and access to resources, but it also reinforced a certain paternalism. It allowed the wealthy to dictate the terms of their giving, maintaining control over how and where their money was used. By funding libraries, schools, and cultural institutions, Carnegie not only shaped the intellectual landscape of America but also crafted an image of himself as a benevolent philanthropist, distancing his legacy from the cutthroat business practices that had built his fortune.

John D. Rockefeller: Strategic Philanthropy and Public Relations

While Andrew Carnegie may have articulated the moral rationale for elite philanthropy, it was John D. Rockefeller who perfected the art of using charitable giving as a tool for managing public perception. As the founder of Standard Oil, Rockefeller built an empire that dominated the oil industry through ruthless business tactics, including price-fixing and leveraging political influence. His practices were so controversial that they led to the eventual breakup of Standard Oil under antitrust laws in 1911.

Public opinion of Rockefeller was, at best, ambivalent and, at worst, hostile. He was often portrayed as a symbol of corporate greed and excess. Yet, over time, Rockefeller rehabilitated his public image through a carefully orchestrated philanthropic campaign. He established the Rockefeller Foundation in 1913, focusing on global health, scientific research, and education. The foundation's work had a significant impact, funding efforts that led to the development of vaccines, the eradication of diseases, and advancements in medical research.

But behind these philanthropic endeavours was a sophisticated public relations strategy. Rockefeller's advisors recognised that charitable giving could soften his image, allowing him to be seen not as a robber baron but as a benefactor of humanity. The Rockefeller Foundation became a model for how elite philanthropy could be used to drive social change and manage the reputation of the ultra-wealthy.

The Paternalism of Elite Giving

One of the most significant features of Gilded Age philanthropy was its inherent paternalism. Industrialists like Carnegie and Rockefeller viewed themselves as superior arbiters of society's needs. Their philanthropy was not about empowering the masses to make their own choices but guiding them toward what the elites considered the "right" path. By funding libraries, museums, and universities, they sought to shape the intellectual and cultural landscape in ways aligned with their values and vision of progress.

This paternalistic approach continues to define elite philanthropy today. Large foundations often dictate the terms of their giving, funding projects that align with their benefactors' interests rather than addressing the needs and desires of the communities they purport to serve. In doing so, these foundations perpetuate a power dynamic in which the wealthy maintain control over the direction of social change, reinforcing their position at the top of the social and economic hierarchy.

Philanthropy as Power Consolidation

The industrialists of the Gilded Age laid the groundwork for what has become a central feature of modern elite philanthropy: the use of charitable giving to consolidate power. By funding educational institutions, scientific research, and global health initiatives, these industrialists created a legacy far beyond their lifetimes.

Their names became synonymous with progress and innovation, even as their business practices continued to shape the economic landscape in ways that benefited the wealthy at the expense of the working class.

In many ways, the philanthropy of the Gilded Age was a precursor to the modern philanthropic-industrial complex, where vast fortunes are channelled into foundations that wield significant influence over public policy, research agendas, and social initiatives. Today, figures like Bill Gates, Jeff Bezos, and Mark Zuckerberg have adopted similar strategies, using their wealth to fund initiatives that align with their personal ideologies and business interests.

The Evolution of Elite Philanthropy

As we look to the present, the legacy of Gilded Age philanthropy is unmistakable. The principles established by Carnegie, Rockefeller, and their contemporaries continue to shape how the ultra-wealthy engage in charitable giving. Today's billionaire philanthropists are not merely seeking to rehabilitate their public image but actively shaping global priorities. For example, foundations like the Gates Foundation have significant influence over global health policies, educational reform, and technological innovation.

Yet, the core dynamic remains the same: elite philanthropy is as much about control as giving. By dictating the terms of their contributions, the wealthy ensure that their influence extends into every facet of society, from politics to science to education. The public sees their largesse and celebrates their generosity, but beneath the surface, philanthropy remains a tool for consolidating power and reinforcing the status quo.

CHAPTER 3

THE CHARITABLE PARADOX: HOW FOUNDATIONS SHELTER WEALTH WHILE PRESERVING POWER

Charity has long been celebrated as a noble act, a gesture of goodwill that transcends self-interest and serves the greater good. At first glance, charitable foundations, often established by the ultra-wealthy, seem to be the pinnacle of altruism—vehicles through which vast wealth is channelled into education, healthcare, and social welfare. However, beneath the veneer of altruism lies a far more complex reality: charitable foundations often act as tax shelters, enabling the ultra-wealthy to avoid paying substantial taxes while maintaining control over enormous resources.

The Birth of the Charitable Foundation: Tax Loopholes and Philanthropic Control

In the early 20th century, as America's wealth gap widened and public opinion soured on the power of monopolies, wealthy industrialists faced growing pressure to give back to society. Figures like John D. Rockefeller and Andrew Carnegie pioneered the concept of the modern charitable foundation, using their vast fortunes to fund philanthropic initiatives. On the surface, these foundations appeared to reflect a newfound commitment to public welfare. However, they also served a dual purpose: they allowed the ultra-wealthy to shelter their wealth from taxes while maintaining control over how their money was used.

The creation of a charitable foundation allows individuals and families to transfer significant portions of their wealth into tax-exempt entities. In the United States, for example, when a billionaire donates assets to their foundation, they can claim a tax deduction for the donation, often reducing their income tax liability significantly. Furthermore, the foundation is exempt from paying income and capital gains taxes, even as its assets grow over time. This system enables the ultra-wealthy to shift resources away from the taxable economy and into a space where they can accumulate wealth tax-free, all under the guise of charitable giving.

The Illusion of Sacrifice: Retaining Control Over Wealth

One of the most striking features of charitable foundations is that, despite the appearance of "giving away" their money, the wealthy founders of these institutions often retain substantial control over the assets. While the foundation is technically a separate legal entity, it is typically governed by a board of directors—many of whom are family members, close associates, or donors. This structure allows the wealthy to continue directing how their money is spent, often in ways that align with their personal or business interests.

Consider the Bill & Melinda Gates Foundation, the largest private foundation in the world. With an endowment of over $50 billion, the foundation has funded critical global health, education, and development initiatives. While its work has undeniably positively impacted millions of lives, it is also worth noting that Bill Gates, through his role in the foundation, continues to wield significant influence over global health policy, technological innovation, and educational reform. This level of control raises critical ethical questions: Is the foundation indeed a force for public good, or is it a means for Gates to shape global priorities in a way that aligns with his vision?

Moreover, foundations are not required to spend the entirety of their assets on charitable causes. In the United States, private foundations must only disburse 5% of their endowment yearly in philanthropic activities. This means that 95% of the foundation's assets can remain invested, often growing in value, while it enjoys its tax-exempt status. This structure allows wealth to be preserved and even expanded within the confines of the foundation, all while evading the taxes that would have been owed had those assets remained in the individual's portfolio.

The Double Standard: Wealth Shelter or Social Benefit?

The use of charitable foundations as tax shelters exposes a troubling double standard. While the ultra-wealthy can shelter their fortunes in these tax-exempt entities, the average taxpayer bears the burden of funding public services like education, healthcare, and infrastructure through income and property taxes. In effect, the tax system is skewed in favour of those who can afford to create foundations, allowing the wealthy to avoid contributing their fair share to the public coffers while claiming credit for their philanthropy.

This dynamic is not lost on critics, who argue that the tax breaks associated with charitable foundations undermine the very notion of democracy. By diverting money that would otherwise be subject to public taxation and oversight, foundations concentrate power in the hands of a select few. Instead of democratic institutions deciding how resources should be allocated—through the public funding of schools, hospitals, and social programs —these decisions are made by private individuals who may prioritise their interests or ideologies.

This consolidation of power is particularly concerning when foundations are used to influence public policy. Many foundations engage in "advocacy philanthropy," where donations are directed toward think tanks, research institutions, or political lobbying efforts to shape legislation. In this way, the wealthy can use their foundations not only to shelter their wealth but also to wield disproportionate influence over the direction of society.

The Evolving Role of Foundations: From Shelter to Influence

Over time, the role of charitable foundations has evolved beyond merely sheltering wealth. Today, they are powerful instruments for shaping societal values, public discourse, and political agendas. Through strategic donations, foundations can influence everything from scientific research to cultural institutions to global development policies. This influence is not always benign, raising critical questions about accountability and transparency.

For example, the Koch family, through its network of charitable foundations, has invested heavily in conservative causes, funding organisations that promote deregulation, climate change denial, and free-market capitalism. By channelling their wealth into these foundations, the Kochs have influenced public policy in ways that align with their business interests while benefiting from the tax advantages associated with charitable giving.

Similarly, the Walton Family Foundation, funded by the heirs of Walmart's fortune, has invested billions in education reform initiatives promoting charter schools and public education privatisation. While these efforts are framed as philanthropic endeavours to improve educational outcomes, critics argue that they also undermine public education and promote a corporate agenda that benefits the Walton family's business interests.

In both cases, we see how charitable foundations can be used to shelter wealth and promote specific political and ideological goals.

This raises important questions about the role of philanthropy in a democratic society: Should the wealthy be allowed to wield such disproportionate influence over public policy simply because they can afford to do so? And does the tax system, by providing incentives for creating foundations, effectively enable the wealthy to evade their responsibilities to the broader society?

Reclaiming the Public Good: Rethinking Philanthropy and Taxation

As charitable foundations continue to increase, it is essential that we critically examine their role in society. While philanthropy can undoubtedly lead to positive social outcomes, we must also recognise how it can be used to perpetuate inequality and consolidate power. One possible solution is to rethink the tax benefits associated with charitable giving. If the goal of philanthropy is truly to serve the public good, then foundations should be held to higher standards of transparency and accountability. This could include increasing the minimum payout requirement, mandating more rigorous reporting on the impact of their activities, and ensuring that foundations are not used as vehicles for political influence.

Additionally, tax policies could be reformed to reduce the ability of the ultra-wealthy to shelter their wealth in foundations. By closing loopholes allowing for the deferral of capital gains taxes or limiting the size of the tax deduction that can be claimed for charitable donations, governments could ensure that the wealthy contribute their fair share to the public treasury.

CHAPTER 4

THE MEDIA'S PHILANTHROPIC LENS: SHAPING PUBLIC PERCEPTION TO FAVOR THE ELITE

In today's information age, media has become the lens through which most public interprets the world. It plays a vital role in shaping opinions, setting social agendas, and determining which narratives deserve attention. But what happens when the same elite funds the media organisations reporting on society's influential figures? In an era where billionaires fund philanthropic initiatives and the media organisations that report on them, a troubling dynamic obscures the reality of wealth, power, and philanthropy. It skews public perception in favour of the elite.

The Symbiotic Relationship Between Media and Wealth

Many major media outlets, particularly nonprofit investigative platforms, depend on funding from philanthropic foundations to sustain their operations. Organisations such as the Gates Foundation, the Ford Foundation, and the Open Society Foundations regularly fund media initiatives, journalistic endeavours, and public information campaigns. While this philanthropy is often framed as a public service aimed at supporting independent journalism and enhancing the free flow of information, it raises critical questions about objectivity and bias.

When media organisations rely on these foundations for funding, they face an inherent conflict of interest. How critical can they be of the individuals and institutions that fund them? A media organisation that depends on grants from a billionaire's foundation is unlikely to publish investigative reports that scrutinise that billionaire's actions or question the broader consequences of their philanthropic activities. This dynamic creates a self-reinforcing cycle in which the media elevates the reputations of philanthropists, framing them as figures of public good while leaving the complexities and darker implications of their power untouched.

For example, through the Gates Foundation, Bill Gates is a prolific funder of media initiatives to promote global health and development issues. Many mainstream outlets, including major newspapers and television networks, have received funding from the Gates Foundation for reporting on these topics. While the foundation's support has undoubtedly expanded coverage of critical global issues, it has also shaped the narrative. The Gates Foundation is often portrayed in overwhelmingly positive terms, with little attention paid to its influence over policy or conflicts of interest, such as its investments in industries that may contradict its philanthropic mission.

The Manufacture of a One-Sided Narrative

Philanthropists and wealthy elites benefit from the media's tendency to focus on their charitable work while ignoring the broader systems of inequality and power that enable their wealth. Media coverage tends to emphasise the positive contributions of philanthropy—such as donations to hospitals, scholarships for underprivileged students, or investments in renewable energy—

without critically examining how these same individuals may have contributed to the very problems their philanthropy aims to address.

This one-sided narrative paints a picture of benevolent wealth, where billionaires are seen as solving society's most significant challenges through generosity. However, in reality, these charitable acts often distract from the systemic exploitation and inequality that allowed the philanthropists to accumulate their fortunes in the first place. A tech magnate who donates millions to climate change initiatives is lauded as a hero, while the media ignores the environmental costs of their industries. A hedge fund manager who funds education reform is praised for their commitment to improving schools. Still, the press rarely questions how their business practices might undermine the economic security of the families those schools serve.

By focusing exclusively on the philanthropic side of the story, the media creates a sanitised version of reality, where wealth is portrayed as inherently good, and the structural inequalities that enable extreme wealth are left unexamined. This skews public perceptions and reinforces the power dynamics that benefit the elite. It sends the message that the ultra-wealthy are essential to solving societal problems, sidelining discussions of how wealth concentration and corporate practices often contribute to these problems in the first place.

The Consequences of a Skewed Media Landscape

The media's reluctance to critically examine elite philanthropy has profound implications for public discourse and democracy. When the public is bombarded with stories about the generosity of the wealthy, it becomes more challenging to engage in a nuanced discussion about the role of wealth in society. The glorification of philanthropy drowns out critical voices questioning whether billionaires should have such outsized influence over public policy or whether their contributions can truly compensate for the social and economic inequalities their wealth represents.

This skewed narrative also perpetuates the myth of the "good billionaire," reinforcing the idea that extreme wealth can be justified if it is used for charitable purposes. In doing so, it obscures the fact that many of the world's wealthiest individuals benefit from tax systems, labour exploitation, and environmental degradation that harm the very communities they purport to help. By creating a media environment that shields the ultra-wealthy from criticism, society loses the opportunity to hold them accountable for their role in perpetuating global inequalities.

Moreover, when media organisations depend on philanthropic funding, they often shy away from stories criticising capitalism, wealth concentration, or policies favouring the rich. Investigative reporting that might expose the darker side of elite influence, such as lobbying efforts, tax evasion, or political donations, becomes scarce. The result is a media landscape largely complicit in promoting the interests of the wealthy while neglecting its responsibility to hold power to account.

The Illusion of Altruism and the Power of Storytelling

It is worth considering the power of storytelling in shaping public opinion. Media outlets craft narratives that reflect the values and priorities of their funders, even if unconsciously. When philanthropists are portrayed as heroic problem-solvers, the public is less likely to demand systemic change. Instead of advocating for more equitable tax policies or stronger regulations on corporate practices, people are encouraged to celebrate individual acts of charity as the solution to society's ills.

This dynamic is particularly evident in how the media frames global development issues. Foundations like the Gates Foundation, which focuses heavily on global health, often shape the narrative around what constitutes progress and success. Their influence over research funding, academic studies, and media coverage means that specific solutions—such as technological interventions or market-driven approaches—are prioritised. At the same time, more radical ideas like wealth redistribution or structural reform are sidelined. The result is a narrow view of social progress that aligns with the interests of the wealthy rather than a holistic understanding of the root causes of inequality.

Media organisations act as the gatekeepers of public perception, determining which stories are told and which are left untold. When the elite funds the gatekeepers themselves, breaking free from a narrative that paints wealth in a favourable light becomes difficult. This dynamic distorts our understanding of philanthropy and limits our ability to imagine alternative systems of social justice that go beyond the benevolent handouts of the rich.

Toward a More Critical and Independent Media

To counteract this trend, we need a more independent and critical media willing to interrogate wealth's role in shaping society. Media organisations must diversify their funding sources to avoid reliance on the very elites they are tasked with scrutinising. Foundations that fund journalism should do so without strings attached, ensuring media outlets retain their editorial independence.

Furthermore, the public must become more sceptical of the narratives that dominate mainstream media. We should question why certain philanthropists receive glowing coverage while others go unexamined, and we should demand greater transparency around how media organisations are funded. By fostering a culture of media literacy and encouraging critical engagement with the stories we consume, we can dismantle the one-sided narrative favouring the elite.

CHAPTER 5

STRATEGIC PHILANTHROPY: THE HIDDEN INFLUENCE OF WEALTH ON SOCIETY'S PRIORITIES

At first glance, philanthropy appears to be a noble endeavour, an act of generosity through which the wealthy contribute to the common good. The image of a benevolent billionaire donating to schools, hospitals, or social causes invokes admiration. But beneath this surface lies a more complex and nuanced reality —one in which strategic donations are wielded not simply for altruistic purposes but as tools to influence education, healthcare, and social policy. Through these donations, wealthy individuals and corporations subtly shape societal priorities, often steering them to align with their personal or corporate interests.

The Power to Shape Society

Philanthropy, particularly at the elite level, is more than an act of giving. It is an exercise in power—a way for wealthy individuals and corporations to exert influence over critical sectors such as education and healthcare, where policies have the potential to reshape entire generations. Under the guise of benevolence, strategic donations allow these elites to subtly dictate priorities, diverting public resources and focusing on issues that align with their agendas.

Education, in particular, has become one of the most potent arenas for the display of philanthropic influence. Through their donations, wealthy donors can shape curricula, introduce new educational models, and fund research that reflects their ideological biases. For example, the charter school movement in the United States owes much of its momentum to the financial backing of wealthy individuals like the Walton family (founders of Walmart) and the Gates Foundation. These philanthropists promote a vision of education reform rooted in market-based solutions, such as school choice and the privatisation of public schools. While these initiatives are framed as innovations designed to improve educational outcomes, they also reflect the broader ideological commitments of their funders—commitments to free-market principles and competition. This philanthropic intervention often undermines public education systems by diverting funds and attention from traditional public schools, raising concerns about equity and access.

The healthcare sector has similarly become a target for strategic philanthropy. Personal or corporate interests often drive donations to hospitals, medical research, and public health initiatives. Pharmaceutical companies, for example, make significant donations to universities and research institutions to fund studies on specific drugs or medical treatments, which can skew the research agenda in their favour. By controlling which projects receive funding, these companies ensure that their products are prioritised, sometimes at the expense of more urgent but less profitable health issues. This influence extends to healthcare policy, where donations from corporate philanthropists can shape decisions about what treatments and services are available to the public.

In education and healthcare, strategic donations allow the wealthy to exert soft power— less overt than political lobbying but no less effective in shaping societal priorities.

The Illusion of Altruism

One of strategic philanthropy's most insidious aspects is how it obscures its true nature. When wealthy individuals or corporations donate to education or healthcare, they are often portrayed as selfless acts of giving. The public is encouraged to view these donations as evidence that the wealthy are using their resources to benefit society. However, the reality is that strategic donations often protect or enhance the donor's interests.

Consider the case of corporate donations to health policy think tanks. While ostensibly intended to support independent research, these donations often come with strings attached. In exchange for financial support, corporate donors may gain a seat at the table, influencing the think tank's research agenda and policy recommendations. This creates a conflict of interest, where the public is led to believe that policy recommendations are based on objective research when, in fact, they may be shaped by the priorities of the donor. For instance, a pharmaceutical company that donates to a think tank researching drug policy may exert influence to ensure that the resulting policies favour its business interests, such as advocating for more extended patent protections or opposing price regulation.

In education, donors frequently use their financial power to promote ideologically driven initiatives. For instance, donors with libertarian leanings may fund educational programs that emphasise individualism and market-based solutions. In contrast, donors with progressive views may support curricula focusing on social justice and equity. Although these donations are presented as a means of improving education, they also reflect the personal beliefs of the donor, shaping the values and priorities imparted to students. In this way, the wealthy can shape what is taught and how future generations perceive the world.

The Consequences of Private Influence on Public Policy

The growing influence of strategic donations on public policy raises profound questions about democracy and equity. At its core, philanthropy allows a small, unelected group of individuals to set the agenda for public institutions. This raises concerns about accountability and transparency, as the priorities of the donor class may not align with the needs or desires of the broader population.

For example, billionaire philanthropists influence global health policy. The Gates Foundation, one of the largest philanthropic organisations in the world, has been instrumental in shaping the international response to infectious diseases such as HIV/AIDS, malaria, and tuberculosis. While the foundation's work in these areas has undoubtedly saved lives, its influence over global health priorities is not without controversy. Critics argue that the Gates Foundation's focus on technological solutions, such as vaccines and pharmaceuticals, has overshadowed broader social determinants of health, such as poverty, inequality, and access to clean water and sanitation. Moreover, the foundation's outsized role in global health governance has raised concerns about privatising public health institutions, with some fearing that decisions about global health priorities are increasingly being made by private donors rather than democratically accountable governments.

In education, the influence of strategic donations has led to the proliferation of charter schools and other market-based reforms that, critics argue, undermine public education. By diverting public funds to run schools privately, these reforms exacerbate existing inequalities, as wealthier students can often access better resources and opportunities than their lower-income peers. This raises important questions about the role of philanthropy in exacerbating, rather than alleviating, social inequalities.

A Call for Greater Accountability

While philanthropy can undoubtedly play a positive role in addressing societal challenges, it is crucial that we critically examine how strategic donations shape public policy. As wealthy donors increasingly wield their financial power to influence education, healthcare, and social policy, we must ensure their influence is subject to democratic oversight. This requires greater transparency in the philanthropic sector and stronger regulations to prevent conflicts of interest and ensure that public institutions remain accountable to the public rather than private donors.

In education, for example, there should be greater scrutiny of how philanthropic donations influence curricula and educational policy. Policymakers must ensure that public schools are adequately funded and that educational reforms are driven by the needs of students and teachers rather than by the ideological preferences of wealthy donors. Similarly, healthcare must have stronger safeguards to prevent corporate interests from shaping research agendas and policy recommendations.

CHAPTER 6

CORPORATE PHILANTHROPY: THE HIDDEN AGENDA BEHIND BRAND GOODWILL

At first glance, corporate philanthropy may seem like a win-win situation. A large company makes a generous donation or invests in a community project, resulting in both the company and society benefit. But beneath this shiny surface of altruism lies a much more complex and often disingenuous strategy. Corporations usually use philanthropy not out of genuine concern for the issues they claim to address but as a calculated tool to bolster their brands, create consumer goodwill, and even open new markets. This type of "philanthrocapitalism" often allows companies to ignore or perpetuate the very problems they pledge to solve.

The Power of Corporate Altruism: A Shield and a Sword

The idea of corporations as philanthropists evokes images of major brands funding clean water initiatives, investing in education, or helping impoverished communities. These narratives dominate corporate social responsibility (CSR) campaigns and public relations materials. But behind the heartwarming stories, there's often a calculated agenda to use philanthropy as a shield against criticism and as a sword to carve out new market opportunities.

Corporate donations, whether they go toward building schools or donating to health causes, are powerful tools for brand building. When a company is seen as generous and socially responsible, it benefits from increased consumer trust, loyalty, and positive media coverage. For example, brands like Coca-Cola and Nestlé have invested millions in clean water initiatives worldwide. While these efforts are widely publicised as benevolent contributions to global welfare, they simultaneously serve as mechanisms to reinforce their brand image as caring and ethical corporations, especially in regions where their products face criticism for contributing to health issues like obesity or environmental degradation. The contradiction here is striking: a soft drink giant that profits from selling sugary beverages invests in clean water projects, gaining goodwill from consumers while avoiding a more complex conversation about its role in global health problems.

Similarly, oil companies like ExxonMobil and BP often invest in renewable energy research and green initiatives while continuing to contribute to the global environmental crisis through their core business activities. These donations create the illusion of corporate responsibility and distract from the more significant, more pressing issues—such as environmental degradation and climate change—that these companies contribute to on a massive scale. In this way, corporate philanthropy becomes a tool for deflection, allowing companies to appear proactive in solving global problems without confronting the root causes of their harmful practices.

Creating Consumer Goodwill: The ROI of Altruism

Corporate philanthropy is often less about the cause and more about the return on investment (ROI) regarding public goodwill. Consumers today, especially younger generations, are increasingly concerned with supporting brands that align with their values. Companies have noticed this shift and, in response, have ramped up their philanthropic efforts to appeal to socially conscious consumers. However, many corporations use philanthropy as a marketing tool to align their brand with prevalent causes rather than address systemic issues or make meaningful changes to their business models.

Consider the case of fast fashion brands like H&M or Zara, which frequently promote their charitable contributions to environmental causes. These companies may donate to reforestation projects or sustainable fashion initiatives. Still, their entire business model relies on the mass production of cheap, disposable clothing that contributes significantly to pollution and waste. By investing in visible philanthropic efforts, these brands can position themselves as eco-conscious while continuing to exploit the very environmental resources they claim to protect. This strategic form of philanthropy allows them to maintain a positive brand image in the eyes of consumers increasingly concerned about sustainability without addressing the fundamental contradictions of their business practices.

In these cases, the ROI of corporate philanthropy is not measured in dollars and cents but in consumer trust and brand loyalty. By associating themselves with prevalent causes, corporations can create a sense of emotional connection with consumers, ensuring that their brand is seen as more than just a profit-driven entity but a force for good in the world. This emotional connection is particularly valuable in an era where a company's perceived ethical stance increasingly drives brand loyalty.

The Market Opportunities Hidden in Charity

One of corporate philanthropy's lesser-discussed but highly significant aspects is its role in opening new markets. Strategic donations often pave the way for companies to expand into underserved areas or new sectors, creating business opportunities under the guise of doing good. This is particularly evident in the tech industry, where major corporations donate hardware, software, or educational resources to schools and communities in developing countries. These donations are typically presented as efforts to bridge the digital divide and provide opportunities to disadvantaged populations. Still, they also serve as a gateway for companies to introduce their products and services into new markets.

For instance, Google and Microsoft have invested heavily in donating technology to schools in developing countries. While these donations undoubtedly provide educational benefits, they also familiarise future consumers with their products. By embedding their software and services into educational systems, these companies ensure that entire generations of students become reliant on their platforms, effectively locking them into their ecosystems. This is not to suggest that these philanthropic efforts are without merit, but they raise important questions about the true motivations behind corporate giving. When philanthropy is tied to market expansion, the line between altruism and self-interest becomes increasingly blurred.

Similarly, pharmaceutical companies frequently donate medications to impoverished regions. While these donations can save lives, they also introduce these companies' products into new markets, often laying the groundwork for future sales. Once a population becomes dependent on a particular drug, the company can leverage that dependency for profit, expanding its market presence under the guise of charitable giving. In this way, philanthropy becomes a strategic tool for market penetration, enabling corporations to enter and dominate new regions without facing the same scrutiny that traditional business expansion might attract.

Ignoring Root Causes: The Limits of Corporate Philanthropy

One of the most troubling aspects of corporate philanthropy is how it often ignores or exacerbates the root causes of the problems it claims to address. By focusing on high-visibility, short-term solutions, corporations can appear to address societal issues without making the systemic changes necessary to create a lasting impact. This is particularly evident in how many corporations approach social justice and inequality.

For example, large corporations may donate to initiatives to reduce poverty or improve education in low-income communities. While these donations can provide temporary relief or opportunities, they often fail to address the underlying economic structures perpetuating inequality. In some cases, corporations even contribute to the very problems they claim to be solving. A company that donates to education initiatives while paying its workers substandard wages, for example, contributes to the poverty cycle it claims to be alleviating. By focusing on charitable giving rather than addressing exploitative labour practices or advocating for systemic economic reform, corporations can avoid taking responsibility for their role in creating or perpetuating social inequities.

CHAPTER 7

PHILANTHROPIC POWER: HOW CHARITABLE FOUNDATIONS SHAPE POLICY FOR PRIVATE GAIN

Beneath the veil of generosity that surrounds many charitable foundations lies an unsettling reality—these institutions, often regarded as altruistic forces for social good, wield immense political power. Through strategic lobbying, donations, and influence campaigns, charitable foundations leverage their financial might to steer political outcomes and shape legislation that aligns with their interests. What is ostensibly a benevolent act of giving becomes, in many cases, a sophisticated tool for controlling public policy, advancing corporate agendas, and securing tax breaks or deregulation.

The Intersection of Wealth and Policy: A Historical Perspective

The entanglement of philanthropic power with political influence is not a new phenomenon. Historically, wealthy industrialists and financiers like John D. Rockefeller and Andrew Carnegie used their foundations to manage their wealth and ensure that their business interests faced minimal government interference. Under the guise of charitable donations, they influenced the regulation of industries they dominated, and even in areas like education or healthcare, their funds helped shape national priorities. By positioning themselves as benefactors of society, these magnates used their financial resources to lobby behind closed doors for favourable legislation, steering policies in ways that benefited their corporate empires.

The foundation model pioneered in the late 19th and early 20th centuries provided an elegant solution to two problems facing these industrialists: it allowed them to safeguard their wealth from inheritance taxes and public scrutiny while giving them an outsized role in shaping society according to their values. This framework has only evolved and expanded in the century since, with modern foundations becoming ever more sophisticated in their approach to lobbying and policy manipulation.

The Quiet Influence of Foundation Lobbying

At the heart of the problem lies the quiet, often invisible nature of how charitable foundations influence political systems. Unlike corporations, whose lobbying efforts are scrutinised and documented, foundations can operate under a more opaque set of rules. They use their donations to fund think tanks, research institutions, and advocacy groups that create a façade of public demand for specific policies. By funding research that aligns with their goals, foundations can create a "knowledge economy" favouring their interests, subtly shifting public discourse and, eventually, the legislative agenda.

Consider the role of large foundations in shaping environmental policy. In many cases, ecological foundations support conservation efforts and sustainability initiatives. However, some have simultaneously pushed for policies favouring specific industries—such as renewable energy or agriculture—where they or their corporate affiliates have significant financial stakes. By backing research or public campaigns that emphasise the need for specific regulations (while ignoring others), foundations can frame the conversation so that their preferred industries receive favourable treatment, tax incentives, or subsidies. This form of influence may not involve directly lobbying politicians, but it is no less potent in shaping the legislative landscape.

Moreover, foundations often work with lobbyists, directing funds toward organisations that can pressure lawmakers more directly. These organisations, ostensibly independent from the foundations themselves, push for regulatory changes or legislative reforms that reflect the goals of their benefactors. This "indirect lobbying" allows foundations to maintain an appearance of neutrality or altruism while still working aggressively behind the scenes to shape policy.

The Case of Educational Reform

Education is a prime example of how charitable foundations influence public policy in ways that serve their long-term interests. The Gates Foundation, for instance, has invested billions into reshaping public education in the United States, mainly through its promotion of charter schools and standardised testing. While these initiatives are framed as efforts to improve educational outcomes, they also align with broader corporate interests—namely, the privatisation of public services and the weakening of teachers' unions, which historically have been significant political opponents of corporate influence in education.

Through its vast network of funding and partnerships, the Gates Foundation has profoundly shaped educational policy, pushing reforms that have led to the proliferation of charter schools, many of which are run by private organisations with corporate ties. By funding research that supports their vision of education reform and providing grants to districts willing to implement their preferred policies, the foundation has been able to circumvent the usual political process, effectively outsourcing public education policy to private interests.

In doing so, the foundation steers the direction of education. It creates new opportunities for corporate profits, as companies involved in standardised testing, educational software, and charter school management benefit from the policies the foundation promotes. What appears on the surface as an altruistic effort to improve public education thus becomes a vehicle for advancing private sector interests under the guise of philanthropy.

Healthcare: Philanthropy and Policy Manipulation

Healthcare policy is another arena where foundations wield considerable influence, often to the detriment of public health. Large healthcare foundations, such as those associated with pharmaceutical companies, have been known to fund lobbying efforts to shape drug approval processes, pricing regulations, and insurance policies to benefit the industry. By directing funds toward advocacy groups that champion specific policy changes —such as expanding access to high-cost medications or fast-tracking drug approvals—these foundations can create a public narrative that appears to be driven by concern for patients but is designed to enhance corporate profitability.

Moreover, foundations often push for healthcare policies that reflect the preferences of their founders or key donors. For instance, a foundation funded by a wealthy individual who opposes government-run healthcare programs might invest in think tanks or advocacy groups that lobby for privatised healthcare models, even if such models increase costs or reduce access to care for vulnerable populations. In this way, charitable foundations can steer healthcare policy in directions that benefit their financial interests or ideological beliefs, often at the expense of broader societal welfare.

The Erosion of Democracy: When Private Interests Dominate Public Policy

The most concerning aspect of this phenomenon is how it erodes democratic processes. When foundations use their financial leverage to influence policy, they effectively bypass the mechanisms of democratic accountability. Elected officials, who are supposed to represent the interests of their constituents, are instead swayed by the research, lobbying, and advocacy funded by wealthy donors. This creates a system in which a small group of individuals, often with vast financial resources, have an outsized role in shaping public policy according to their preferences and interests.

This is particularly troubling in areas such as environmental policy, where foundation-backed research can push for solutions that align with corporate interests rather than addressing the systemic causes of environmental degradation. Similarly, in healthcare and education, foundations can advance policies that benefit their donors or corporate affiliates while ignoring the needs of the broader public.

In essence, what we see is a privatisation of public policy. Instead of policy being shaped by the needs and desires of the electorate, it is increasingly being dictated by the interests of a wealthy few, operating under the guise of philanthropy. This not only undermines the principles of democracy but also skews public policy in favour of corporate interests, exacerbating inequality and eroding public trust in the institutions that are supposed to serve them.

CHAPTER 8

THE PRICE OF KNOWLEDGE: HOW PHILANTHROPIC DONATIONS SHAPE EDUCATION, MARGINALISE THE UNDERSERVED, AND PRIORITISE THE ELITE

Education, the cornerstone of societal progress and individual empowerment, has long been seen as the pathway to opportunity and success. Yet, in the hallowed halls of some of the world's most prestigious educational institutions, philanthropic donations often shape the forces that should drive equality and advancement. While ostensibly given to improve the quality of education and expand access, these donations frequently wield a more insidious form of power—one that reshapes curriculum, directs research priorities, and even alters admissions policies in ways that prioritise elite students over underserved populations.

The Philanthropic Influence on Curriculum

At the heart of education lies the curriculum—a framework that defines the scope of knowledge and the perspectives imparted to students. However, when educational institutions become beholden to large donations from philanthropists, the curriculum can be shaped not by society's needs or students' intellectual growth but by wealthy donors' interests. What should be a neutral and academically rigorous structure can morph into a tool that reflects the ideologies and priorities of the financial elite.

For example, specific donations to universities have been tied explicitly to creating endowed professorships or establishing new academic departments in recent years. These endowments often come with strings attached: donors may stipulate that their funds only be used to support research or courses that align with their personal or corporate interests. In one notable case, the Koch Foundation, associated with the libertarian billionaire Koch brothers, has donated millions of dollars to universities across the U.S. with the express condition that its funding be used to promote free-market economics. This financial influence has led to the proliferation of economics departments and research centres that espouse a particular ideological bent, often at the expense of alternative viewpoints.

This phenomenon not only narrows the intellectual diversity within educational institutions but also perpetuates a form of ideological gatekeeping. Students are funnelled into a worldview that serves the interests of the donor class. At the same time, critical perspectives on issues such as wealth inequality, corporate regulation, and environmental sustainability may be sidelined or underfunded. Once a battleground of ideas, the curriculum becomes a marketplace where the highest bidder dictates the terms of intellectual inquiry.

The Impact on Research Priorities

Donor influence extends far beyond curriculum and into the realm of research. In a perfect world, academic research would be driven by the quest for knowledge, the needs of society, and the betterment of humanity. Yet, when large donations come with conditions, research priorities can be skewed toward projects that serve corporate interests or reflect the preferences of wealthy individuals.

Consider the field of biomedical research. Donations from pharmaceutical companies or wealthy individuals with financial stakes in certain medical technologies often direct research funding toward areas that promise financial returns. While this can result in groundbreaking innovations, it can also distort the allocation of resources, diverting funding away from critical but less profitable areas of study. Research into rare diseases, mental health, or public health issues affecting marginalised communities may be overlooked in favour of projects with transparent commercial applications.

The same dynamic plays out in environmental research, where donors with ties to the fossil fuel industry may fund studies that downplay the impacts of climate change or promote "greenwashed" technologies that allow corporations to maintain their profit margins without addressing systemic environmental damage. The public, unaware of the financial strings attached to research, assumes that scientific inquiry is unbiased when it is often shaped by the invisible hand of wealth.

This narrowing of research priorities limits the scope of academic inquiry and has broader societal consequences. When universities, which are supposed to be bastions of independent thought and innovation, align their research agendas with the interests of the wealthy, they contribute to a system that prioritises profit over public good.

Admissions Policies and the Reinforcement of Elitism

Perhaps the most direct and troubling way donations shape educational institutions is through their impact on admissions policies. Elite universities, particularly in the United States, are notorious for granting preferential treatment to the children of wealthy donors—a practice that has come to be known as "legacy admissions." In return for significant financial contributions, these universities often admit students from wealthy families, even if their academic qualifications fall short of the institution's typical standards. This practice reinforces elitism and perpetuates a cycle in which wealth begets privilege, and privilege begets more wealth.

At the same time, students from underserved communities—those who could benefit most from the opportunities provided by elite education—are left behind. Even when institutions claim to value diversity and inclusivity, the financial incentives created by donations often result in admissions policies that favour the wealthy. Students from low-income backgrounds, students of colour, and those from rural or underserved urban areas are frequently sidelined in favour of applicants with financial or familial connections to the institution.

This trend has far-reaching implications for social mobility. Education is supposed to be the great equaliser, providing a path out of poverty and into positions of influence and success. Yet, when elite institutions prioritise the children of the wealthy, they reinforce existing power structures and limit the potential for upward mobility. The result is a two-tiered system in which the rich and well-connected secure their positions at the top while the rest compete for scraps.

The Marginalization of Underserved Populations

The influence of donations on curriculum, research, and admissions policies culminates in the marginalisation of underserved populations. While elite students benefit from tailored curriculums, cutting-edge research opportunities, and preferential admissions, students from disadvantaged backgrounds often find themselves excluded from these benefits. In many cases, the very issues affecting these populations—such as income inequality, racial discrimination, or access to affordable healthcare—are sidelined in favour of topics that align with the interests of the wealthy donors who fund the institutions.

Moreover, when donations are directed toward programs or initiatives that purport to serve underserved populations, they often come with conditions that limit their effectiveness. For instance, scholarships funded by donations may have strict eligibility requirements that exclude many students in need, or they may be awarded in ways that prioritise merit over need, further disadvantaging low-income applicants. Similarly, programs aimed at improving access to education for marginalised communities may be underfunded or deprioritised in favour of initiatives that generate more positive publicity for the institution and its donors.

In this way, philanthropic donations exacerbate existing inequalities within the education system, creating a landscape in which the wealthy not only maintain their privilege but actively shape the future of education to ensure their continued dominance.

The Illusion of Altruism

Philanthropy, particularly in education, is often framed as selflessness—an expression of the wealthy's desire to give back to society and improve the world for future generations. Yet, as this essay has shown, donations to educational institutions frequently serve a more calculated purpose. Far from being acts of pure altruism, these donations allow wealthy individuals and corporations to shape the institutions that produce the next generation of leaders, ensuring that their values, interests, and power structures remain intact.

The influence of donations on curriculum, research, and admissions policies reveals the double-edged nature of philanthropy in education. While donations can undoubtedly improve resources, facilities, and opportunities for students, they also come with significant strings attached. These strings, often invisible to the public, pull the institutions in directions that serve the interests of the elite at the expense of intellectual diversity, social mobility, and the needs of underserved populations.

CHAPTER 9

THE POLITICS OF AID: HOW LARGE FOUNDATIONS SHAPE DEVELOPMENT IN THE GLOBAL SOUTH

In the sprawling landscapes of the Global South, where development challenges intertwine with centuries of colonial exploitation, a new form of influence has emerged—one that masquerades as benevolence but often replicates the imbalances of the past. Large foundations, wielding billions in resources, are increasingly at the centre of development projects to improve infrastructure, health, and education in developing countries. Yet, beneath the surface of this charitable giving lies a more complex and, at times, troubling reality. These foundations often dictate the terms of development, shaping policies, controlling resources, and guiding the direction of progress in ways that disproportionately benefit donor countries and multinational corporations.

The Rise of Philanthropic Powerhouses

The 21st century has seen an unprecedented rise in the power of private philanthropy, with large foundations such as the Bill & Melinda Gates Foundation, the Rockefeller Foundation, and the Ford Foundation taking on roles that were once the purview of governments and multilateral institutions. These organisations often position themselves as agents of global good, funding initiatives to combat poverty, improve healthcare, and foster economic growth in the Global South. However, the scale of their financial contributions significantly influences how development is conceived, planned, and executed.

For instance, in the healthcare sector, the Gates Foundation has invested billions in efforts to eradicate diseases such as malaria and polio in sub-Saharan Africa. While these efforts have yielded undeniable public health benefits, they also raise questions about who sets the global health agenda and whose interests are ultimately served. By controlling the purse strings, these foundations can determine which issues receive attention, which research gets funded, and which solutions are prioritised—all while sidestepping democratic accountability.

The Hidden Agenda: Economic and Political Leverage

One of the most significant criticisms of large foundations is their tendency to serve donor countries' economic and geopolitical interests, particularly the United States and other Western powers. When these foundations fund development projects, they often do so in ways that open up markets for multinational corporations or promote policies that align with the strategic objectives of their home nations. This creates a troubling dynamic in which the Global South becomes a testing ground for new technologies, agricultural systems, and economic models that benefit external actors more than local communities.

For example, foundations' role in promoting genetically modified (GM) crops in Africa. The Gates Foundation has strongly advocated adopting GM agriculture funding research and development projects across the continent. While proponents argue that GM crops can help address food security challenges, critics point out that these initiatives often serve the interests of multinational agribusiness companies such as Monsanto (now

Bayer), which stand to profit from the sale of patented seeds and chemical inputs. Moreover, the push for GM agriculture can undermine traditional farming practices and erode local food sovereignty, leaving smallholder farmers dependent on expensive, foreign-produced technologies.

In this way, development projects funded by large foundations can act as a Trojan horse for the expansion of Western corporate power. Under the guise of promoting economic growth and food security, these initiatives can entrench dependency on external actors, stripping local communities of their agency and ability to shape their development trajectories.

The Problem of Policy Capture

In addition to their influence over development projects, large foundations exert considerable control over policy decisions in the Global South. This phenomenon, known as "policy capture," occurs when private interests—whether corporate or philanthropic—shape public policy in ways that prioritise their objectives over the needs and desires of the broader population.

One of the most glaring examples of policy capture can be seen in the education sector. Foundations such as the Gates Foundation and the Chan Zuckerberg Initiative have funnelled significant resources into education reform in countries across Africa and Latin America. These efforts often focus on promoting standardised testing, data-driven performance metrics, and using digital technologies in classrooms. While these reforms may align with the foundations' vision of modern, efficient education systems, they often fail to consider the local cultural and social contexts in which they are implemented. Moreover, by tying development funding to specific policy changes, these foundations effectively undermine the sovereignty of governments in the Global South, pressuring them to adopt policies that may not be in the best interests of their citizens.

The revolving door between philanthropic organisations and government institutions further amplifies the influence of large foundations on policy. Many high-ranking officials within large foundations come from government backgrounds, while others take up influential positions in national or international policymaking bodies. This blurring of the lines between public and private sectors creates fertile ground for policy capture, as foundations can use their financial leverage to steer public policy in directions that align with their strategic goals.

The Double-Edged Sword of Conditional Aid

The funding provided by large foundations is often conditional, meaning that recipient countries must meet certain criteria or adopt specific policies to receive financial support. While these conditions are framed as necessary to ensure the effectiveness of development projects, they also reinforce the power dynamics between donor foundations and recipient countries. Conditional aid allows foundations to dictate the terms of development, effectively stripping local governments and communities of their agency.

This can be particularly problematic in healthcare, where foundations such as the Gates Foundation have been central in shaping global health policies. For example, the Gates Foundation has been instrumental in promoting vertical healthcare programs—those that focus on specific diseases, such as HIV/AIDS or malaria—rather than horizontal programs that strengthen healthcare systems. While vertical programs can be highly effective in combating individual diseases, they can also divert resources and attention away from broader public health initiatives, leaving healthcare systems ill-equipped to handle other pressing challenges.

In countries with weak public health infrastructures, the focus on vertical programs can exacerbate existing inequalities, as resources are concentrated on specific diseases or populations rather than being distributed equitably across the healthcare system. Moreover, by tying funding to particular policy changes, foundations can limit the ability of local governments to set their healthcare priorities, further entrenching the power dynamics between donor countries and the Global South.

The Illusion of Local Ownership

One of the most insidious aspects of the influence wielded by large foundations is the illusion of local ownership. While these foundations often frame their development projects as partnerships with local governments, NGOs, and communities, the reality is that the donor organisations frequently dictate the terms of these partnerships. Local actors may have little say in the design, implementation, or evaluation of development projects, even as they are tasked with carrying out the work on the ground.

This lack of local ownership can lead to development initiatives poorly suited to the needs and realities of the communities they are intended to serve. Projects may be designed based on the assumptions and priorities of donors rather than on a deep understanding of local contexts. As a result, development efforts can fail to achieve their intended outcomes, or worse, they can exacerbate existing problems by imposing inappropriate or unsustainable solutions.

Moreover, the lack of local ownership can undermine the long-term sustainability of development projects. When external actors drive initiatives with little input from local communities, there is often little buy-in or commitment to maintaining these projects once the initial funding dries up. As a result, development efforts may have only temporary or superficial impacts, leaving underlying issues unresolved.

A Path Forward: Rethinking Development in the Global South

If development in the Global South is to be truly equitable and sustainable, it must be rooted in local ownership, accountability, and transparency. While large foundations can play an essential role in funding development initiatives, their influence must be tempered by greater democratic oversight and the meaningful involvement of local communities in decision-making processes. This means rethinking the terms of philanthropic giving, moving away from conditional aid and policy capture toward a model that prioritises local needs, knowledge, and agency.

One potential solution is to strengthen the role of multilateral institutions, such as the United Nations or the World Health Organization, in coordinating development efforts. While far from perfect, these institutions are more accountable to the global community than private foundations and can help ensure that development projects are aligned with the needs of recipient countries rather than the interests of donor countries or corporations.

Another solution is to promote greater transparency in the relationships between foundations, governments, and corporations. By shining a light on the financial ties between these actors, we can begin to hold them accountable for how they shape development in the Global South. This includes tracking how funds are allocated, who benefits from development projects, and how these initiatives impact local communities.

Finally, we must empower local communities to take a more active role in shaping their development trajectories. This means investing in capacity-building and supporting grassroots organisations that can advocate for the needs and rights of marginalised populations. We can only begin to create a more just and equitable global development system by centring the voices of those most affected by development projects.

CHAPTER 10

THE CHARITABLE ILLUSION: HOW DONATIONS MASK THE HARMFUL PRACTICES OF THE HEALTHCARE INDUSTRY

In healthcare, where the stakes are often life and death, the image of benevolent pharmaceutical companies donating to medical causes can seem like a balm for a troubled system. On the surface, these acts of charity are heralded as noble efforts to eradicate disease, promote public health, and advance medical research. Billions of dollars flow into healthcare foundations, research institutions, and global health initiatives, often under the auspices of philanthropy. Yet, behind this veil of generosity lies a more insidious reality: many of the same companies that donate to healthcare are also the architects of the problems they purport to solve. By contributing to charitable causes, they deflect attention from their harmful practices and maintain a public image of compassion and responsibility—while profiting handsomely from the system's dysfunction.

The Philanthropic Façade

Pharmaceutical and medical companies often present themselves as champions of public health, funding initiatives that target diseases such as cancer, diabetes, and infectious diseases like HIV/AIDS. These donations are often showcased in glossy public relations campaigns, with executives making grand announcements about their companies' commitment to saving lives and improving global health outcomes. However, this carefully curated image of corporate benevolence conceals the darker reality that many companies are simultaneously engaged in practices that harm the people they claim to help.

One prominent example is the opioid crisis in the United States. For years, pharmaceutical companies like Purdue Pharma, the makers of OxyContin, aggressively marketed highly addictive opioids while downplaying their dangers. As the crisis spiralled into a public health emergency, these same companies began donating to addiction treatment centres and opioid recovery programs. The irony is staggering: corporations that fueled the opioid epidemic with misleading marketing and irresponsible distribution practices are now profiting from its aftermath, using charitable donations to present themselves as part of the solution rather than the cause. By funding recovery programs, they position themselves as compassionate actors in the fight against addiction, all while evading accountability for their role in creating the problem.

Profiting from the Problem

The pharmaceutical industry's involvement in healthcare philanthropy is not solely about image management—it is also a means of maintaining control over the narrative and ensuring that their profit-making strategies remain unchallenged. By funding research and healthcare initiatives, pharmaceutical companies can steer the direction of medical advancements and policy decisions in ways that align with their corporate interests.

Consider, for instance, the issue of drug pricing. Many pharmaceutical companies donate to patient advocacy groups and research foundations, ostensibly to help improve access to life-saving medications. Yet, at the same time, these companies engage in price-gouging practices that make these medications unaffordable to many patients. The exorbitant cost of insulin, a drug that has been around for nearly a century, is a glaring example. Insulin manufacturers have come under fire for raising prices to such an extent that some patients have been forced to ration their doses or forgo treatment altogether, with devastating consequences.

In response to public outrage over these practices, pharmaceutical companies have donated to diabetes research and patient support organisations, positioning themselves as part of the solution to the crisis they helped create. While helpful in the short term, these donations do little to address the root cause of the problem: the unchecked power of pharmaceutical companies to set drug prices at will. By controlling the flow of charitable funds, these companies divert attention away from systemic issues such as drug pricing reform, ensuring their profit margins remain intact while projecting an image of altruism.

The Exploitative Cycle of Crisis and Charity

At the heart of this dynamic is a vicious cycle: pharmaceutical and medical companies profit from creating or exacerbating public health crises then use charitable donations to present themselves as part of the solution. This cycle is particularly evident in global health, where pharmaceutical companies often donate to initiatives to tackle diseases in developing countries. On the surface, these efforts appear to be altruistic contributions to global well-being. However, a closer examination reveals that these donations often expand markets and entrench corporate power in vulnerable regions.

Take, for example, the global campaign to combat malaria. Pharmaceutical companies have donated millions to organisations working to distribute antimalarial drugs and bed nets in sub-Saharan Africa. While these efforts have undoubtedly saved lives, they also serve to maintain a dependency on pharmaceutical interventions rather than addressing the underlying causes of malaria outbreaks, such as inadequate infrastructure, poverty, and environmental degradation. Moreover, by focusing on drug distribution, pharmaceutical companies ensure a steady stream of profits from the sale of antimalarial medications, perpetuating a cycle in which the disease is managed but never truly eradicated.

This same dynamic plays out in the realm of vaccines. Companies like GlaxoSmithKline and Pfizer donate millions to global vaccination efforts, particularly in regions where infectious diseases remain a significant threat. These donations are often hailed as acts of corporate social responsibility, yet they also open up new markets for vaccine sales. These companies sometimes exert considerable influence over global health organisations, shaping vaccination policies and priorities to benefit their bottom line. For instance, by promoting certain vaccines over others, pharmaceutical companies can ensure that their products remain the standard of care in developing countries, even when cheaper or more effective alternatives may be available.

The Ethics of Healthcare Philanthropy

At its core, the issue of charitable donations in the healthcare sector raises fundamental questions about the ethics of corporate philanthropy. Can a company be considered benevolent when its business practices contribute to the problems it claims to address through charity? Or are these donations merely a form of damage control—a way to deflect criticism while continuing to engage in harmful behaviours?

The answer lies in understanding the power dynamics at play. By controlling the flow of charitable funds, pharmaceutical and medical companies can shape public perceptions of their role in healthcare. They dictate which issues receive attention, which research gets funded, and which solutions are pursued. In doing so, they ensure that the status quo remains intact—one in which they can continue to profit from a broken healthcare system while masking their complicity in its failures.

Moreover, these donations often come with strings attached. In some cases, pharmaceutical companies use their financial leverage to influence the research agenda of academic institutions or the policy positions of advocacy groups. This creates a troubling conflict of interest, as organisations that rely on corporate donations may hesitate to criticise the companies that fund them. As a result, meaningful reform—whether in drug pricing, regulatory oversight, or healthcare access—becomes more difficult to achieve.

A Call for Accountability

There must be greater transparency and accountability in how these funds are used to address the ethical challenges posed by charitable donations in the healthcare sector. This means shining a light on the financial ties between pharmaceutical companies, medical institutions, and advocacy groups and ensuring that donations do not come at the expense of systemic reform. It also means holding companies accountable for their business practices rather than allowing them to use philanthropy as a shield against criticism.

In the case of drug pricing, for example, pharmaceutical companies should not be allowed to deflect attention from their price-gouging practices by donating to patient support programs. Instead, there should be more significant pressure on these companies to lower prices and ensure that life-saving medications are accessible to all patients, regardless of income. Similarly, in the realm of global health, pharmaceutical donations should not be used as a substitute for addressing the root causes of disease outbreaks. Instead, there should be a concerted effort to invest in infrastructure, education, and poverty alleviation so that developing countries are not perpetually dependent on external aid.

Ultimately, the goal of healthcare philanthropy should be to improve health outcomes in a sustainable and equitable way—not to perpetuate the profit-driven motives of pharmaceutical and medical companies. By demanding greater accountability and transparency, we can begin to break the cycle of crisis and charity and work toward a healthcare system that truly serves the needs of all people.

CHAPTER 11

THE GREEN MIRAGE: HOW ENVIRONMENTAL PHILANTHROPIES SHIELD POLLUTERS AND STUNT REAL CLIMATE ACTION

In an age where climate change looms as an existential threat, the public has become increasingly attuned to environmental issues, scrutinising corporations and governments for their role in perpetuating ecological destruction. In response, some of the world's largest companies—top polluters—have made high-profile donations to environmental causes, pledging to invest in sustainability and reduce their carbon footprints. They launch foundations, fund climate research, and back conservation initiatives while painting themselves as part of the solution. But behind this eco-friendly façade lies a troubling reality: many of these environmental philanthropies, funded by corporations with enormous environmental footprints, serve not to drive meaningful climate action but to protect corporate interests. By diverting attention from the core of the problem—corporate pollution and exploitation of natural resources—these initiatives mask ongoing environmental damage while allowing corporations to profit from the crises they claim to address.

The Rise of Corporate Green Philanthropy

Over the last two decades, environmental philanthropy has experienced unprecedented growth, as some of the largest corporations in the world—many of them in industries like oil, mining, and agriculture—have dedicated billions to ostensibly "green" causes. This surge in corporate giving appears to be a much-needed boost to the environmental movement. After all, if the world's biggest companies are dedicating their resources to fight climate change, progress is on the horizon.

However, a closer look reveals that these philanthropies are not purely altruistic. Instead, they are carefully orchestrated campaigns designed to present polluting corporations as environmental stewards. Companies like ExxonMobil, BP, and Chevron, which have long histories of contributing to ecological degradation, fund environmental foundations that advocate for market-friendly climate policies—those that often delay or water down regulations that could meaningfully curb emissions. These companies claim to be committed to sustainability while lobbying against the policies that could hold them accountable for their emissions and ecological destruction.

This contradiction lies at the heart of corporate green philanthropy. While these companies make headlines for their environmental donations, they continue to engage in practices that exacerbate the climate crisis. Their contributions to environmental foundations often function as little more than a public relations tool, allowing them to project an image of corporate responsibility without addressing their role in fueling the problem.

The Greenwashing Machine

Greenwashing—misleading the public into believing a company is more environmentally friendly than it is—has become an integral part of corporate environmental philanthropy. By funding ecological initiatives, these companies effectively co-opt the language of sustainability, making it difficult for the public to discern between genuine environmental efforts and those designed to protect corporate interests.

For instance, major oil companies have spent millions on "sustainability" campaigns and donations to environmental organisations. Yet, they continue to expand fossil fuel extraction, invest in new oil projects, and lobby against clean energy policies. Through carefully crafted messaging and charitable donations, they deflect attention from the scale of their environmental impact, convincing the public and regulators alike that they are part of the solution rather than the problem. This dynamic allows corporations to buy goodwill while doubling down on the practices that accelerate climate change.

Nowhere is this clearer than in the case of plastic pollution? Large corporations like Coca-Cola and Nestlé, some of the world's top plastic polluters, have pledged millions to environmental organisations that combat plastic waste. These companies are champions of ocean cleanup initiatives and recycling programs while continuing to flood the market with single-use plastics. Their donations to environmental foundations effectively shield them from public scrutiny, diverting attention from the systemic issues that fuel the plastic crisis. Instead of addressing the root cause—excessive plastic production—these companies promote recycling efforts that shift the responsibility for managing waste onto consumers and local governments.

Controlling the Environmental Narrative

One of the most insidious aspects of corporate-funded environmental philanthropies is their ability to shape the narrative around climate action. By controlling the flow of charitable funds, polluting companies ensure that environmental initiatives align with their corporate agendas. This means that specific solutions, such as market-based approaches like carbon trading, receive ample funding and attention. At the same time, more radical measures, like stricter regulations on emissions or a move away from fossil fuels, are sidelined.

For instance, many of the most significant environmental foundations advocate for carbon offset programs, in which companies can "offset" their emissions by investing in projects like reforestation or renewable energy. While these programs may sound promising, they often serve as a smokescreen for continued pollution. Rather than reducing their emissions at the source, companies can purchase offsets, allowing them to maintain business as usual while claiming to be "carbon neutral." This market-friendly approach to climate action does little to address the systemic changes needed to decarbonise the economy. Still, it allows corporations to present themselves as environmentally responsible without fundamentally altering their practices.

Moreover, corporate-funded environmental foundations often lobby against policies that would impose stricter regulations on polluting industries. This creates a conflict of interest: organisations relying on corporate donations may hesitate to push for policies that could alienate their benefactors. As a result, bold climate solutions—such as ending fossil fuel subsidies, implementing carbon taxes, or banning plastic production—are often left off the table.

The Impact on Global Environmental Justice

Corporate environmental philanthropies' influence extends far beyond donor countries' borders, with particularly devastating effects on the Global South. Many of the world's most vulnerable communities bear the brunt of climate change, yet corporate-funded environmental initiatives often marginalise their needs and voices. These initiatives frequently prioritise market-based solutions that benefit multinational corporations while ignoring the needs of communities on the frontlines of environmental destruction.

Take, for example, the issue of land conservation. Many corporate-funded environmental philanthropies advocate for creating protected areas in the Global South, where ecosystems are preserved and human activity is restricted. While these initiatives may sound laudable, they often lead to the displacement of Indigenous and local communities who have lived in harmony with these ecosystems for generations. These communities are forced off their land in the name of conservation while multinational corporations continue to extract resources from nearby areas with impunity.

In this way, corporate environmental philanthropies reinforce existing power imbalances, allowing the world's wealthiest companies and countries to profit from the natural resources of the Global South while claiming to protect the environment. This green colonialism, masked by the rhetoric of conservation and sustainability, allows corporations to maintain their control over the global environmental agenda, all while perpetuating the very inequalities that drive ecological degradation in the first place.

A Call for Genuine Climate Action

The rise of corporate environmental philanthropies reveals a troubling truth: the companies that contribute most to the climate crisis also control the conversation about how to solve it. By funding ecological initiatives, these corporations deflect attention from their harmful practices and steer the global climate agenda in ways that benefit their bottom line.

Suppose we are to address the climate crisis in a meaningful way. In that case, we must look beyond the surface of corporate green philanthropy and demand real accountability from the world's biggest polluters. This means pushing for policies that hold corporations responsible for their environmental impacts—such as strict emissions regulations, bans on single-use plastics, and an end to fossil fuel subsidies—rather than allowing them to offset their pollution through charitable donations. It also means supporting grassroots environmental movements, particularly those led by marginalised communities, that advocate for systemic change rather than market-based solutions.

At its core, the climate crisis is a crisis of power: the power of multinational corporations to shape the global environmental agenda in ways that protect their interests. If we are to create a sustainable and just future, we must reclaim that power and demand that environmental philanthropy serve the planet's needs rather than the profits of the few.

CHAPTER 12

THE PARADOX OF POWER: HOW LARGE NONPROFITS BECOME TOOLS FOR THE ELITES THEY WERE MEANT TO CHALLENGE

Nonprofit organizations have long been heralded as the moral compass of modern society, created to address pressing social issues, champion the marginalized, and counterbalance the excesses of capitalist and governmental systems. Its mission is rooted in the pursuit of justice and equality—offering a vehicle for social progress by tackling poverty, inequality, environmental degradation, and systemic injustice. Yet as these organizations grow more significant, more influential, and more reliant on elite funding, a curious transformation takes place: many begin to mirror the power structures they were once established to challenge.

Over time, these nonprofits find themselves entrenched in the systems that sustain the elites they ostensibly oppose. The rise of large, well-funded nonprofit organizations often reveals a troubling paradox. Though they exist to confront societal issues, they inadvertently become tools for consolidating power, benefitting the wealthy and influential while offering only piecemeal solutions to the problems they were designed to solve.

The Origins of Philanthropic Ambition

The initial impulse behind nonprofit organizations is often noble and genuine. Grassroots movements with limited resources form the bedrock of many of these institutions, driven by passionate individuals determined to make a difference. Their founders are frequently outsiders to systems of power—activists, social workers, educators, and community organizers—seeking to remedy the failings of existing institutions. Their goals are ambitious: to dismantle poverty, rectify racial injustice, halt environmental collapse, or bring attention to issues overlooked by profit-driven industries and indifferent governments.

However, as these organizations grow in size and scope, their financial needs increase exponentially. This is where the cycle of entrenchment begins. Large foundations and wealthy benefactors start to see these nonprofits as opportunities not just for social good but for influence. As the influence of elite donors grows, so does the potential for nonprofits to lose sight of their original mission.

Elite Capture and Mission Drift

The phenomenon of "elite capture" explains how these organizations, initially founded to challenge entrenched power, become co-opted by the systems they sought to disrupt. As nonprofits expand, they require funding on a much larger scale, often from private philanthropists, corporate sponsors, or government grants. These donors—typically the wealthiest individuals and institutions—hold disproportionate sway over the organization's trajectory. In exchange for financial support, donors often push nonprofits to pursue initiatives aligned with their personal interests or corporate agendas, creating an insidious form of mission drift.

The rise of elite-dominated boards further exacerbates this dynamic. To attract substantial donations, many large nonprofits invite corporate executives, financiers, and even political insiders to sit on their boards. While this increases access to wealth and resources, it erodes the organization's ability to take bold, transformative action. After all, how can a nonprofit challenge economic inequality if its board members represent the same industries responsible for that inequality? How can a nonprofit advocate for environmental sustainability if its major donors profit from resource extraction?

The result is a subtle but significant shift in priorities. Rather than pursuing systemic change, large nonprofits settle for incremental reforms that don't fundamentally threaten the status quo. In many cases, they become focused on maintaining their financial viability rather than taking risks that could alienate wealthy donors. Thus, the very elites responsible for social and environmental harm become the architects of the solutions proposed by these nonprofits.

The Illusion of Progress

One of the most pernicious effects of elite capture is the illusion of progress. Large nonprofits are adept at producing polished reports, staging high-profile events, and showcasing their achievements to the media. They have professional marketing teams, PR consultants, and access to policymakers—all of which allow them to position themselves as social change leaders. But often, this evident progress is superficial. While nonprofits may celebrate individual success stories or boast about metrics demonstrating impact, they rarely address the underlying causes of the problems they purport to solve.

Take the issue of global poverty. Large international nonprofits have spent billions of dollars on poverty reduction programs, many of which have provided tangible benefits to impoverished communities. However, they often do so without questioning the global economic systems perpetuating inequality. Structural issues like tax avoidance by multinational corporations, the exploitation of cheap labour in the Global South, or the environmental degradation caused by resource extraction are rarely on the agenda. Instead, nonprofits focus on more palatable initiatives like micro-loans, which may lift individuals out of poverty without addressing the broader systemic factors keeping entire populations impoverished.

The same is true for environmental nonprofits. Many organizations that receive funding from polluting industries promote market-based solutions to climate change, such as carbon trading schemes, that allow corporations to continue polluting while claiming environmental responsibility. By framing these solutions as innovative and forward-thinking, nonprofits create the illusion of progress while failing to push for the radical changes—such as stricter regulations or a shift away from fossil fuels—that are urgently needed.

The Gatekeeping of Social Change

As large nonprofits become more bureaucratic and dependent on elite funding, they often adopt a gatekeeping role, determining which issues are worthy of attention and which solutions are feasible. This gatekeeping function further entrenches the power of elites, allowing them to steer the conversation around social issues in ways that protect their interests.

For example, wealthy donors may be more inclined to support nonprofits focused on issues like education or healthcare—causes that, while important, are less likely to challenge their economic power. At the same time, nonprofits focused on wealth redistribution, labour rights, or anti-capitalist organizing struggle to secure funding. In this way, the priorities of large nonprofits become aligned with those of the wealthy, reinforcing existing power dynamics rather than dismantling them.

Additionally, many large nonprofits actively discourage more radical forms of activism, fearing that confrontation with powerful interests could jeopardize their funding or political access. Activists who call for more aggressive action on issues like climate justice, racial inequality, or corporate accountability are often marginalized within the nonprofit world, their voices drowned out by the more moderate positions of well-funded organizations.

Reclaiming Nonprofit Power

While the rise of large, elite-funded nonprofits presents significant challenges, it also offers reflection and reform opportunities. Like any other institution, the nonprofit sector is not immune to the corrupting influence of money and power. However, it is also a space where grassroots movements can challenge these dynamics and push for meaningful change.

To reclaim the transformative potential of nonprofits, we must question the role of elite funding in shaping social movements. This means advocating for greater transparency and accountability within the sector, ensuring nonprofits remain accountable to their communities rather than the wealthy individuals who fund them. It also means supporting smaller, community-based organizations more likely to take bold, systemic action without fear of alienating wealthy donors.

Ultimately, nonprofits must return to their roots as agents of social justice, unafraid to challenge entrenched power and demand radical change. This will require a shift in how we think about philanthropy—not as a tool for the wealthy to assuage their guilt or protect their interests, but as a vehicle for collective action and systemic transformation.

CHAPTER 13

THE PROFIT MOTIVE IN SCIENCE: HOW CHARITABLE FOUNDATIONS SHAPE RESEARCH AND INNOVATION

Scientific research and technological innovation are often seen as forces for the common good—tools to advance knowledge, improve health, solve societal challenges, and build a better future for all. However, behind this idealized vision lies a more complicated reality, in which the priorities of scientific discovery are increasingly driven by the financial imperatives of those who fund it. Charitable foundations, often hailed as champions of public welfare, play a significant role in shaping research direction. Yet, while these organizations project an image of benevolence, their funding choices frequently steer advancements in ways that prioritize profit over public good.

As the lines blur between philanthropy and private interests, it is essential to scrutinize how charitable foundations, particularly those with deep ties to corporate wealth, influence the course of science and technology. In doing so, we must ask critical questions: Who decides which research is funded? What are the long-term consequences of prioritizing profit-driven innovations? And how do these decisions affect the broader societal pursuit of knowledge and progress?

The Illusion of Altruism in Scientific Funding

Funding scientific research has always been a complex interplay of government, private sector, and philanthropic contributions. Historically, government agencies like the National Institutes of Health (NIH) or National Science Foundation (NSF) have provided the bulk of support for basic research—long-term studies without immediate commercial applications but with profound implications for future discoveries. In recent decades, however, the role of charitable foundations has grown considerably. Foundations with vast financial resources, such as the Gates Foundation or the Wellcome Trust, now significantly sway global research priorities.

On the surface, this influx of philanthropic capital appears to be a positive development. After all, if governments struggle to meet the financial demands of scientific inquiry, why shouldn't private foundations step in to fill the gap? Yet, the motives behind such generosity deserve closer examination. Far from being disinterested benefactors, many foundations are linked to corporate empires, raising questions about whose interests are being served by their investments in research.

The Profit Motive in Medical and Technological Research

Nowhere is the influence of charitable foundations more pronounced than in the medical field, where research funding often directs the trajectory of pharmaceutical and biotechnological advancements. The Gates Foundation, for instance, has poured billions of dollars into global health initiatives, from vaccine development to disease eradication efforts. While such initiatives have undeniably saved lives, they have also skewed research priorities favouring treatments that promise commercial viability.

One glaring example is the disproportionate focus on diseases prevalent in wealthy countries, where patients can afford costly treatments, compared to conditions affecting poorer regions. While diseases like cancer and diabetes receive substantial funding, neglected tropical diseases that primarily impact the Global South continue to languish in relative obscurity. This disparity is not coincidental; it reflects that pharmaceutical companies—many of which receive significant foundation support—prioritize research that will yield profitable drugs and treatments. The foundations' role in guiding these priorities is often overlooked but cannot be ignored.

Moreover, technological innovation in healthcare, particularly in areas like gene editing, artificial intelligence (AI) in diagnostics, and personalized medicine, has become a key focus for many foundations. These advancements hold immense promise but also carry risks of deepening inequalities. As foundations invest in patent and marketable cutting-edge technologies, the resulting products often come with exorbitant price tags, accessible only to the wealthiest segments of society. In this sense, the supposed altruism of foundation-backed research becomes a mechanism for profit generation that leaves the most vulnerable populations behind.

Engineering a Future for the Few

Beyond the healthcare sector, charitable foundations' influence extends into artificial intelligence, energy, and environmental science. For example, foundations tied to tech giants increasingly fund AI research, shaping the future of automation, machine learning, and data science. Yet, these investments are frequently guided by the same corporate interests that dominate the technology sector. Innovations in AI are often framed as solutions to societal challenges—whether in healthcare, climate change, or education—. Still, many such technologies are designed to serve the interests of corporations that can monetize them.

Consider the rise of AI-powered surveillance technologies. Some foundations have backed research in AI ethics, ostensibly to explore the responsible use of these tools. Yet, at the same time, these foundations invest in tech companies developing surveillance systems for profit. The tension between ethical concerns and financial interests becomes starkly apparent when the same tools used to monitor citizens are marketed to authoritarian governments or employed in the service of corporate security.

Similarly, foundations linked to fossil fuel wealth in the energy sector have attempted to rebrand themselves as leaders in clean energy innovation. They fund research into carbon capture technology or renewable energy sources while continuing to invest in industries that contribute to environmental degradation. The result is a skewed form of environmental philanthropy that emphasizes technological fixes over systemic change—preserving the status quo rather than addressing the root causes of the climate crisis. These foundations profit from the problem and the supposed solutions, creating a circular system of influence where the public good is subordinated to corporate gain.

Steering the Ethical Compass

One of the most concerning aspects of foundation-driven research is its capacity to steer the ethical discourse surrounding scientific and technological advancements. When foundations fund the research and the moral debates that accompany it, they position themselves as arbiters of what is right and just in innovation. They fund conferences, ethics boards, and policy discussions, shaping the public narrative in ways that protect their financial interests while appearing socially responsible.

This influence can be subtle but powerful. For instance, the discourse around AI ethics often focuses on issues like data privacy or algorithmic bias—undoubtedly significant concerns—but seldom delves into more radical questions about the societal implications of mass automation or the concentration of AI power in a few corporations. By framing the debate in specific ways, foundations can deflect attention from more disruptive questions that challenge their influence.

The same holds for the biotech and pharmaceutical sectors. Foundations heavily involved in genetic research often support discussions around the ethical use of CRISPR and gene editing, framing these debates around safety and regulation. Yet, there is far less attention paid to the broader societal implications of a future where genetic enhancements are accessible only to the wealthy, leading to a potential stratification of society based on genetic privilege.

The Future of Scientific Innovation

The influence of charitable foundations on scientific research and technological innovation raises pressing questions about the future of these fields. As foundations continue to dominate research agendas, we must remain vigilant about how profit motives can undermine the public good. The question is not whether foundations should fund scientific research—after all, private capital can play an essential role in advancing knowledge—but how we ensure that this funding aligns with society's broader interests rather than a select few's financial interests.

To address this, greater transparency is essential. Foundations must be open about their investments, ties to corporate interests, and long-term goals. We must also advocate for a more equitable distribution of research funding, ensuring that basic science—without immediate commercial applications—is not neglected in favour of profit-driven ventures. Public funding for research must be strengthened so that the wealthiest donors do not dictate the direction of scientific progress.

Ultimately, the future of scientific research and technological innovation should not be for sale. The promise of science is its ability to expand human knowledge and improve the quality of life for all, not just those who can afford the latest innovations. To safeguard this promise, we must hold foundations accountable and ensure their investments serve the public good—rather than merely enriching those who already have the reins of power.

CHAPTER 14

DYNASTIES OF GENEROSITY: HOW ELITE FAMILIES PRESERVE POWER THROUGH CHARITABLE GIVING

In its idealized form, charitable giving is an act of altruism—a gesture of goodwill meant to alleviate suffering, support communities, and create lasting positive change. However, this narrative becomes more complex when examined through the lens of elite families and their philanthropic pursuits. For the wealthiest families in the world, charitable giving is often more than an expression of benevolence. It is a tool of influence, a means of perpetuating their legacy, and, most significantly, a mechanism for preserving power across generations. In the guise of philanthropy, these families maintain control over industries, politics, and society, creating a system where their influence remains entrenched, often under the radar.

Using charitable giving to safeguard dynastic control is not new, but its subtlety and sophistication have evolved. Through strategic philanthropy, elite families ensure their place in the present and future, crafting a narrative of public-spirited generosity while quietly shaping the world in ways that benefit their interests.

The Transformation of Wealth into Influence

For elite families, wealth is not static. It must be constantly managed, protected, and, perhaps most importantly, transformed into influence. Philanthropy provides a unique vehicle for this transformation. By establishing charitable foundations, these families demonstrate their commitment to social causes and create enduring institutions that reflect their values, protect their legacies, and ensure their ongoing relevance in key areas of public life.

Consider the Rockefeller, Ford, and Carnegie families—household names associated with American industry, whose fortunes were built during the Gilded Age and early 20th century. Their philanthropic efforts, through organizations like the Rockefeller Foundation, the Ford Foundation, and the Carnegie Endowment for International Peace, have enormously impacted education, health, and international development. While these contributions to society are undeniable, they also reinforce the family's influence over key sectors of society.

By funding universities, research institutes, and public policy think tanks, these families gain a direct line to forming knowledge and public discourse. Through charitable foundations, elite families can steer academic research, direct public conversations on global issues, and ensure that their economic, political, or social ideologies remain influential. The legacy of these foundations outlasts the individuals who created them, ensuring that future generations of the family can inherit not just wealth but an institutionalized form of influence.

Power in Perpetuity: The Role of Foundations

One of the most effective ways elite families preserve power through philanthropy is by establishing charitable foundations in perpetuity. Unlike direct donations to specific causes or short-term grants, foundations are structured to last indefinitely, allowing elite families to sustain their influence across generations. By setting the terms of the foundation's mission and priorities, family members—present and future—can shape the direction of their charitable giving while retaining control over how their wealth is used.

These foundations often operate with boards of trustees that include family members or close associates, ensuring that the values and interests of the founding family are upheld. Moreover, through careful management and investment of their endowments, foundations grow in wealth over time, allowing them to exert even more significant influence as their assets multiply.

The Gates Foundation, for example, has positioned itself as one of the most potent philanthropic entities in the world, directing billions of dollars toward global health, education, and poverty alleviation. But beyond its contributions to these causes, the foundation represents a legacy for the Gates family, enabling them to shape global policy and international development for generations. The foundation's influence over public health—such as its role in global vaccine distribution—shows how philanthropic institutions can become powerful actors on the world stage, with the potential to shape entire industries and governmental policies.

Philanthropy as Public Relations: Shaping Legacy and Image

Another dimension of elite philanthropy is its function as a tool for public relations. For elite families, charitable giving serves to craft a public image that balances out or even erases negative perceptions of their wealth and business practices. By aligning themselves with social causes and charitable initiatives, these families can distance themselves from the darker aspects of their economic dominance, using philanthropy to construct a legacy of positive impact.

Take, for instance, the Sackler family, whose fortune was built on Purdue Pharma and its controversial marketing of the opioid OxyContin. Thanks to their generous donations to museums, galleries, and academic research, the family has long been associated with prestigious cultural institutions and universities. Through these philanthropic contributions, the Sacklers cultivated a reputation as patrons of the arts and education—until their connection to the opioid crisis scrutinised their charitable endeavours.

While the Sackler case is an extreme example, it illustrates a broader trend: philanthropy is often used to "launder" reputations, transforming families with controversial business histories into champions of social progress. Charitable donations provide a way for elite families to shape their legacy, ensuring that they are remembered not for the harm they may have caused through their business dealings but for their positive contributions to society. The public narrative of their impact becomes carefully curated, reinforcing their status as benevolent forces for good.

Exclusion Through Inclusion: Reinforcing Inequality

At its core, philanthropy by elite families can paradoxically reinforce the inequalities it seeks to address. While charitable giving ostensibly aims to tackle social issues such as poverty, inequality, and lack of access to education, it often does so in ways that maintain the structures of power that benefit the wealthy. Through their foundations, elite families may choose to fund programs that provide temporary relief to those in need. Still, they rarely support initiatives that challenge the systemic causes of inequality—such as tax policies, labour laws, or corporate regulation—that allow them to retain their wealth and influence.

Moreover, the vast wealth accumulated by elite families often allows them to influence the allocation of public resources. When a foundation funds a particular initiative—scientific research, educational reform, or public health programs—it effectively privatizes decisions that would otherwise fall within the purview of democratically elected governments. In doing so, elite families can sidestep public accountability and steer social progress in directions that align with their interests, all under the guise of charitable giving.

In this sense, elite philanthropy functions as a form of "exclusion through inclusion." By engaging in high-profile charitable efforts, elite families are benefactors in the social fabric. Still, they do so in ways that exclude others from decision-making. Their philanthropy becomes a means of maintaining control—over institutions, industries, and the direction of societal change—while perpetuating a system that privileges the wealthy.

CHAPTER 15

THE ILLUSION OF BENEVOLENCE: HOW SMALL CHARITABLE GESTURES DISTRACT FROM HARMFUL PRACTICES

In a world dominated by headlines that praise corporate philanthropy and wealthy individuals for their charitable gestures, it is easy to overlook the dissonance between the good deeds they broadcast and the darker realities they obscure. From multinational corporations funding community programs to billionaires donating to food banks, the narrative of corporate and individual generosity often masks the damaging practices that fuel their wealth. While seemingly noble, these small acts of charity frequently serve as strategic diversions from environmental harm, labour exploitation, and political manipulation—practices that undermine the very causes these acts purport to support.

The Strategic Nature of Charitable Giving

At first glance, charitable donations—whether from financial support to education, healthcare, or community initiatives—seem like acts of kindness that come from a genuine desire to give back to society. But beneath this veneer of goodwill lies a deeper, more calculated strategy. For corporations and the wealthy elite, philanthropy is a tool used to create a positive public image and, more importantly, to shield themselves from criticism.

Consider, for example, the oil and gas industries. These corporations are some of the most significant contributors to environmental degradation and climate change, but many have established charitable foundations or community outreach programs to promote environmental sustainability. ExxonMobil, one of the largest oil companies in the world, frequently donates to conservation efforts and sponsors ecological initiatives. But these gestures do little to mitigate the reality that the company's core business—extracting and burning fossil fuels—continues to contribute significantly to the climate crisis. The small charitable donations function as a distraction, allowing the company to claim social responsibility while sidestepping accountability for its role in environmental destruction.

Similarly, tech giants like Amazon and Facebook have made headlines for donations to social causes, from pandemic relief to education initiatives. Yet these acts of generosity obscure harmful business practices, such as poor working conditions, anti-union tactics, and data privacy violations. Amazon's highly publicized donations during the COVID-19 pandemic, for example, were contrasted with reports of warehouse workers being forced to work in unsafe conditions without adequate protection. In this context, charitable contributions are not signs of corporate altruism but attempt to divert attention from labour exploitation and maintain a favourable public image.

The Psychology of the "Feel-Good" Gesture

Charitable giving, particularly when widely publicized, psychologically impacts the public. It creates what social psychologists call the "halo effect"—the tendency to favourably view a person or organization based on a single positive trait or action. In this case, the charitable act becomes the positive trait that overshadows more harmful behaviours.

Billionaires like Warren Buffett and Bill Gates have famously pledged large portions of their wealth to charitable causes through initiatives like the Giving Pledge. This has earned them widespread admiration as philanthropists using their wealth for the greater good. Yet this narrative often omits that their fortunes were amassed through systems that contribute to economic inequality, exploit labour markets, and influence political decisions. By donating billions to charity, these individuals can cultivate a public image emphasising their benevolence, distracting from how their business empires have reinforced the social problems their donations are meant to solve.

These gestures' "feel-good" nature plays a key role in perpetuating this illusion. When a corporation donates to a local food bank or sponsors a school, it generates positive press coverage, boosting its reputation as a socially responsible entity. Seeing the charitable act, the public is less likely to scrutinize the company's labour practices, environmental impact, or political lobbying efforts. In essence, the small gesture of charity acts as a smokescreen, obscuring the organisation's broader, more damaging behaviours.

Charity as a Shield for Political Influence

One of the most insidious ways charitable gestures are used to deflect criticism is in the realm of political influence. Corporations and wealthy individuals often engage in philanthropy to soften the public's perception of their political activities, mainly when lobbying for policies that serve their interests at the expense of the public good.

Take, for example, the pharmaceutical industry, which has long been criticized for its role in driving up drug prices and lobbying against healthcare reforms. Major pharmaceutical companies frequently donate to healthcare-related causes, sponsoring medical research or supporting public health campaigns. However, these charitable donations are often overshadowed by the industry's aggressive lobbying efforts to protect their profits by opposing legislation making healthcare more affordable. The philanthropic contributions create the illusion that these companies are committed to improving public health, while in reality, they are working behind the scenes to ensure that their profits are prioritized over patient care.

Similarly, political donations and charitable contributions often go hand-in-hand for wealthy individuals who seek to influence policy. By making high-profile donations to social causes, these individuals create a positive public image that can help deflect criticism of their political activities. For instance, a billionaire who donates to climate change research may also be funding political candidates who oppose environmental regulations. The charitable donation becomes a form of reputation insurance, allowing the individual to continue exerting political influence while maintaining the appearance of social responsibility.

The Paradox of "Doing Good" While Doing Harm

The most troubling aspect of these small charitable gestures is the paradox they create—where entities actively engaged in harmful practices are also positioned as saviours through their philanthropy. This paradox allows corporations and wealthy individuals to maintain their power and undermines the very causes they claim to support.

When corporations donate to environmental causes while simultaneously polluting the planet, or when billionaires fund education initiatives while profiting from systems that perpetuate economic inequality, the result is a superficial form of social responsibility. It allows the public to feel good about these entities' contributions without addressing the structural issues that need to be solved.

Moreover, this paradox reinforces a dangerous cycle in which the problems created by corporate practices—environmental degradation, labour exploitation, and economic inequality—are used to justify further corporate control. Corporations and wealthy individuals are the only ones capable of solving the problems they helped create, using their wealth and influence to shape public discourse and policy to serve their interests.

CHAPTER 16

CHALLENGING THE MONOPOLY OF ELITE PHILANTHROPY: THE RISE OF GRASSROOTS MOVEMENTS AND ALTERNATIVE MODELS

In recent years, the traditional model of philanthropy—dominated by elite donors, wealthy individuals, and corporate foundations—has faced increasing scrutiny. While billionaires are celebrated for their charitable giving, often framed as heroic benefactors solving global crises, a deeper examination reveals an unsettling concentration of power. As it has largely existed, Philanthropy has allowed the ultra-wealthy to dictate social change, controlling where and how resources are distributed while reinforcing their influence and interests.

Against this backdrop, grassroots movements and alternative philanthropic models have emerged as a powerful counterforce. These community-led initiatives, born out of frustration with elite control, challenge traditional philanthropy's paternalism and top-down decision-making. They advocate for a more democratic, decentralized approach that empowers communities to address social issues on their own terms, ensuring that those most affected have a say in shaping the solutions.

The Limits of Traditional Philanthropy

At its core, traditional philanthropy often replicates the very inequalities it seeks to solve. Most philanthropic donations come from a small group of ultra-wealthy individuals or corporate entities. While their contributions can undoubtedly make an impact—building schools, funding medical research, or alleviating poverty—their approach is frequently transactional. Elite donors, sitting atop global wealth, determine the priorities, leaving the recipients of charity with little to no agency in how resources are allocated. The relationship between donor and beneficiary is one of dependency, in which the wealthy maintain control over social solutions. At the same time, those on the ground are treated as passive aid recipients.

The problem with this model is not just the imbalance of power but also the narrow scope of the solutions offered. Elite-driven philanthropy often prioritizes issues palatable to the donor class—education reform, technological innovation, or global health initiatives—while neglecting more systemic issues like wealth inequality, labour rights, and environmental justice, which might threaten their economic interests. Moreover, elite donors frequently view social problems through a technocratic lens, favouring short-term, quantifiable results over long-term, structural change.

This approach also allows the wealthy to avoid addressing the root causes of inequality and injustice. For instance, a billionaire who profits from exploitative labour practices or environmental degradation may donate large sums to fight poverty or fund conservation efforts. However, these charitable acts, while well-intentioned, often mask the harmful practices that generated their wealth in the first place. The result is a philanthropic system that reinforces the status quo, offering incremental improvements without challenging the deeper structural forces that sustain inequality.

The Rise of Grassroots Movements

In response to these limitations, grassroots movements have gained momentum, advocating for a shift in philanthropy's operations. These movements reject the top-down approach of elite donors and emphasize the importance of community-led decision-making. At their core, grassroots initiatives believe those closest to the problem are also closest to the solution. By empowering marginalized communities to take control of the resources and tools needed to address social issues, these movements offer a more democratic, inclusive, and sustainable philanthropy model.

One example of grassroots philanthropy can be seen in the growing popularity of mutual aid networks. Mutual aid is not new—it has deep roots in communities of colour, working-class neighbourhoods, and other marginalized groups that have long been excluded from traditional systems of support. Mutual aid networks operate on principles of solidarity rather than charity, with community members pooling resources to meet each other's needs directly. Whether organizing food banks, providing housing support, or offering healthcare services, mutual aid is built on reciprocity, trust, and shared power.

During the COVID-19 pandemic, mutual aid networks experienced a resurgence as governments failed to provide adequate support and traditional philanthropic institutions struggled to respond effectively. Communities worldwide organized to care for one another, distributing food, medical supplies, and financial assistance without waiting for approval or funding from elite donors. In this context, mutual aid demonstrated the power of grassroots, decentralized philanthropy in times of crisis, offering a powerful counter-narrative to the traditional, hierarchical model of giving.

Another example is the Participatory Grantmaking movement, which places decision-making power directly in the hands of the communities being served. Participatory grantmaking challenges the idea that donors or foundations should control where funding goes, instead creating processes in which community members —often those most impacted by social issues—make funding decisions themselves. This approach not only democratizes philanthropy but also ensures that resources are allocated in ways that reflect the actual needs and priorities of the community.

Participatory grantmaking is being implemented by foundations such as the Disability Rights Fund, which provides grants to disabled persons' organizations in the Global South. By involving disabled individuals in the decision-making process, the fund ensures that resources are directed toward projects that genuinely address the needs and concerns of those most affected by disability rights issues. Similarly, the Brooklyn Community Foundation has adopted a participatory grantmaking model, allowing community members in Brooklyn, New York, to determine where grants should go, ensuring that funding reflects the realities on the ground.

Alternative Models: Solidarity-Based Philanthropy

Beyond grassroots movements, some alternative philanthropic models focus on solidarity rather than charity. Solidarity-based philanthropy is rooted in the belief that philanthropy should not be about "giving back" but rather about redistributing power and wealth in ways that challenge the systemic inequalities that perpetuate social issues.

One prominent example of this model is the concept of "Just Transition," which originated within the labour and environmental justice movements. Just Transition focuses on shifting away from extractive industries, like fossil fuels, to regenerative, community-centred economies. In the context of philanthropy, Just Transition calls for funding models that support frontline communities—those most affected by environmental and economic injustices—while addressing the root causes of inequality and ecological destruction.

Solidarity-based philanthropy also calls for a fundamental shift in wealth accumulation and distribution. Rather than relying on the benevolence of the wealthy to give back a portion of their profits, this model advocates for systemic changes that would prevent such extreme concentrations of wealth in the first place. This might include higher taxes on the wealthy, stronger labour protections, and policies that promote economic and environmental justice.

In addition, models like community foundations and giving circles offer ways for individuals, particularly those without access to wealth, to pool resources and support causes they care about. Giving circles, for instance, allows groups to come together, each contributing a small amount of money and collectively deciding how to distribute their funds. This model democratizes philanthropy, ensuring that individuals at all income levels can participate in giving and that decisions are made collectively rather than by a single donor.

The Significance of Grassroots and Alternative Models

The rise of grassroots movements and alternative philanthropic models represents a profound shift in how we think about addressing social issues. These models challenge the paternalism and control of elite donors, advocating for a more democratic, community-led approach that centres on the voices and needs of those most impacted by social problems. By rejecting the notion that the wealthy know best, grassroots movements emphasize the importance of shared power, collaboration, and long-term, systemic change.

Moreover, these models are significant because they expose the limitations of traditional philanthropy. Elite-driven philanthropy, while often well-intentioned, tends to focus on band-aid solutions that do not address the root causes of inequality. Grassroots and alternative models, by contrast, offer a more holistic approach that provides immediate support and seeks to transform the systems that perpetuate injustice in the first place.

At a time when wealth inequality is at an all-time high and communities worldwide are grappling with the effects of climate change, economic instability, and social unrest, the need for more equitable, democratic approaches to philanthropy has never been more urgent. By empowering communities to take control of their destinies, grassroots movements and alternative philanthropic models offer a path toward a more just, sustainable, and inclusive future—one where philanthropy is not about the power of the few but the collective power of the many.

CHAPTER 17

PHILANTHROPY AT A CROSSROADS: REFORMING CHARITY TO SERVE THE PUBLIC GOOD

In its idealized form, Philanthropy is a noble endeavour—a tool by which society's most privileged can give back, addressing the needs of the less fortunate and supporting initiatives that drive positive social change. Yet, as the world has evolved, so has the nature of charitable giving, which is increasingly becoming a mechanism through which the wealthy consolidate their power. Rather than simply serving the public good, philanthropy often becomes a vehicle for maintaining control, shaping policy, and burnishing reputations. This presents a fundamental question: Can philanthropy be reformed to serve the public good genuinely, or is it inextricably tied to the interests of the elite?

In this concluding reflection, I explore the nuances of reforming modern philanthropy. Drawing on both the criticisms of the current system and the potential for change, I offer possible solutions for creating more transparent, equitable giving systems that prioritize collective benefit over elite influence.

The Problem: Philanthropy as Power Consolidation

At its core, philanthropy suffers from an inherent paradox: It allows the wealthy to position themselves as society's saviours, who benefit from the structures that perpetuate inequality. In many cases, the problems philanthropists seek to address are byproducts of the capitalist systems from which they have profited. This can be seen in various sectors, from education and healthcare to environmental causes, where philanthropy often offers temporary relief without tackling the root causes of these issues.

Consider the role of charitable foundations in influencing public policy. Through their foundations, elite donors often steer research, advocacy, and policy development in ways that align with their interests. The Gates Foundation, for instance, has had a profound impact on global health and education initiatives. Still, critics argue that its interventions sometimes prioritize technological solutions that align with corporate interests over more sustainable, community-led approaches. Similarly, charitable contributions to political campaigns and lobbying efforts by wealthy donors allow them to exert disproportionate influence over the democratic process, often undermining the principles of equality and fairness that philanthropy purports to uphold.

Philanthropy's tax-exempt status only deepens these concerns. The ultra-wealthy can shield significant portions of their wealth from taxation by establishing charitable foundations, effectively transforming public revenue into privately controlled assets. This creates a twofold issue: it deprives governments of resources that could be used for public welfare programs and allows the wealthy to dictate how those resources are used. In this sense, philanthropy is a tool for perpetuating inequality, as the rich maintain their wealth and power while appearing to act in the public interest.

A Path to Reform: Transparency and Accountability

Whether philanthropy can be reformed to serve the public good hinges on two key principles: transparency and accountability; without greater transparency in how philanthropic funds are distributed and the motives behind those decisions, philanthropy will continue to be viewed with scepticism. A more open system would allow the public to scrutinize where money is going and the real impact of donations, ensuring that philanthropy is more than just a public relations exercise for the wealthy.

One potential solution lies in the implementation of stronger regulations surrounding philanthropic giving. Governments could establish stricter requirements for charitable foundations, mandating that they disclose the specific outcomes of their donations and any potential conflicts of interest. For example, suppose a foundation funded by a fossil fuel company is making donations to environmental causes. In that case, there should be transparency regarding how those funds are used and whether they genuinely advance sustainability or merely deflect attention from the company's harmful practices.

Moreover, philanthropic organizations should be held accountable for the long-term impact of their donations, not just their immediate outputs. Too often, philanthropy is evaluated based on short-term, quantifiable outcomes, such as the number of vaccines distributed or schools built, rather than the more significant, systemic changes needed to address the root causes of societal issues. By focusing on long-term accountability, philanthropy could shift from a reactive model to one that proactively works to dismantle the systems of inequality it seeks to address.

Democratizing Philanthropy: Community-Led Giving

Another avenue for reform is the democratization of philanthropy. The rise of grassroots movements and participatory grantmaking has shown that there are alternative models of giving that empower communities rather than perpetuate elite control. These models are based on the belief that those closest to the problems can also develop solutions. By providing communities direct control over how philanthropic funds are used, these models ensure that resources are directed toward initiatives that reflect the needs and priorities of those most affected.

Participatory grantmaking, in particular, has gained traction to redistribute power in philanthropy. In this model, foundations cede decision-making authority to the communities they serve, allowing them to determine how grants should be allocated. This ensures that philanthropic funds are used in ways that align with the needs of marginalized populations and foster greater trust between donors and recipients. When people have a say in how resources are distributed, they are more likely to be invested in the success of those initiatives, leading to more sustainable and impactful outcomes.

Moreover, community foundations and giving circles represent a growing trend toward collective philanthropy. These models allow individuals, particularly those without vast wealth, to pool their resources and collectively decide how to distribute funds. By democratizing philanthropy in this way, we can create systems of giving that are more inclusive, equitable, and reflective of the diverse needs of society.

Reimagining Philanthropy: From Charity to Solidarity

Ultimately, the most profound reform of philanthropy may lie in shifting the ethos underpinning charitable giving. Rather than viewing philanthropy as a benevolent act of charity in which the wealthy give back to the poor, we must reimagine it as solidarity—a recognition that we are all interconnected and that actual social change requires collective action.

This shift from charity to solidarity would require philanthropists to move beyond traditional forms of giving and engage in more transformative practices that challenge the structures of power and inequality. For example, philanthropists could support initiatives that advocate for living wages, workers' rights, and economic justice rather than simply donating money to alleviate poverty. Rather than funding technological solutions to climate change, they could invest in grassroots movements fighting for environmental justice and the rights of Indigenous peoples.

In this reimagined model of philanthropy, the role of the donor is not to "save" those in need but to stand in solidarity with them, using their resources to support movements already working to create a more just and equitable world. This requires a fundamental shift in thinking about wealth, power, and responsibility. It requires philanthropists to recognize that their wealth is not a symbol of virtue but a product of systems that have enabled their success at the expense of others. It requires them to listen, to learn, and to share power with those who have been historically marginalized.

ABOUT THE AUTHOR

Dr Karthik K is a distinguished academic, researcher, and author passionate about unravelling complex societal dynamics. With a Ph.D. and M.S. from IIT Madras, his career spans more than a decade of critical inquiry, thought leadership, and interdisciplinary exploration. His work often bridges the technical and the societal, offering fresh perspectives on the intersection of power, policy, and progress.

In The Dark Side of Philanthropy, Dr. Karthik ventures into the intricate world of charitable giving, deconstructing the narratives surrounding elite philanthropy. Drawing on meticulous research and a sharp analytical lens, he challenges the reader to rethink the true impact of modern charity. The book reflects his commitment to exposing systemic inequities and advocating for transformative, community-led change.

Dr. Karthik's diverse professional background, including roles in academia, industry, and nonprofit collaboration, uniquely positions him to analyze the intricate interplay of power and influence. As a seasoned writer, he has authored books and research articles that resonate with readers seeking clarity, depth, and actionable insights. His expertise spans topics from computational fluid dynamics to the societal implications of technological and philanthropic systems.

When not writing or researching, Dr. Karthik mentors emerging innovators and supports grassroots initiatives to create equitable, sustainable futures. He lives in Tamil Nadu, India, where he continues to question, challenge, and inspire change.

www.ingramcontent.com/pod-product-compliance
Lightning Source LLC
Chambersburg PA
CBHW050329230526
45471CB00005B/2413